Great Collectors' Cars

Great Collectors' Cars
by Gianni Rogliatti

GROSSET & DUNLAP
A FILMWAYS COMPANY
Publishers • New York

The illustrations reproduced in this book were supplied by the following organizations and photographers, to whom the publishers are grateful: Associated Press, Josip Ciganovic, The Deutsches Museum, l'Editrice dell'Automobile archives, Hamlyn Group archives, Indianapolis Motor Speedway Museum, Giorgio Lotti, Henri Malartre Collection, Museo Storico Alfa Romeo, Museo Nazionale della Scienza e della Tecnica Leonardo da Vinci, The National Motor Museum, Gianni Rogliatti, Julius Weitmann.

Preceding pages: a 1909 Rolland-Pilain, a 1911 Léon Bollée Double Berline and a 1913 Clément Bayard outside the Rochetaillée museum.

Right: the National Motor Museum 1898 Canstatt-Daimler

Pages 10 and 11: the National Motor Museum 1902 De Dietrich

First published in the United States in 1973 by Grosset & Dunlap, 51 Madison Avenue, New York 10010

Copyright © 1970 by L'Editrice dell'Automobile; originally published in Italian under the title of *Le Piu'Belle Vettura D'Epoca;* copyright © English-language edition Arnoldo Mondadori Editore 1973; published in 1973 by The Hamlyn Publishing Group Limited under the title of *Period Cars*
All rights reserved

Published simultaneously in Canada

Library of Congress Catalog Card No.: 72-79968

ISBN: 0-448-01914-0

Third printing 1978

Printed and bound in Italy by Mondadori, Verona

CONTENTS

CONSERVATOIRE NATIONAL DES ARTS ET METIERS

Situated in the heart of Paris, only a few steps from the junction of the Boulevard Sebastopol and the Rue Réaumur, the Conservatoire National des Arts et Metiers is one of the world's most famous science museums. Its land transport section, with a subdivision devoted to road vehicles, is only a part of the whole collection.

The Conservatoire is not only a museum and documentation center, producing its own publications, but also a school of applied sciences. Since 1901 it has also been the National Laboratory, carrying out tests for controls and measures for French industry.

Its site was originally occupied in the 9th century by the Priory of St. Martin-des-Champs. This was destroyed by the Normans, but it was rebuilt in 1060, when it passed into the hands of the Cluny order. The church, which was completed in the 12th century and remains in excellent repair today, serves to house the road vehicle section of this great museum.

When the Conservatoire was established

PARIS

in 1799, most of the present buildings were already standing. Only a few additions were made later, although much went into adapting the buildings to their present purposes; the 13th-century refectory, for example, became a library. The buildings retain a solemn air, and the style remains predominantly that of Paris of the 17th and 18th centuries.

The road transport exhibits are relatively few, but of outstanding historic importance. They include the manual vehicle made by Vaucanson, the famous 18th-century engineer; Cugnot's remarkable steam *fardier* of 1770, the true precursor of the power-driven horseless carriage, which was designed to draw heavy artillery; Bollée's famous *L'Obéissante* steam carriage of 1873, and important examples of de Dion, Serpollet, and other pioneers. There are also horse-drawn vehicles, bicycles, important engines and engine components such as carburetors and magnetos. The museum authorities are now planning for some important modern vehicles.

Apart from automobiles, the somber halls and long corridors of the Conservatoire are literally crammed with material from the history of science and engineering. In the famous echo room on the ground floor can be seen the instruments used by the great chemist Lavoisier; elsewhere are sections on astronomy, clocks and watches, metallurgy, and even early flying machines, suspended as if in flight.

The first floor is devoted to mechanical sources of power, from the windmill to steam engines, and includes the extremely rare relics of Pascal, among them his remarkable calculating machine. Technologies such as weaving, typography, photography, radio and television, physics, optics and acoustics are all represented. On the second floor there is a section containing telegraphic and telephonic apparatus. A meteorological section is of particular interest since the metric decimal system originated in France, based on calculations of the curve and measurement of the earth's meridian.

Cugnot Fardier

1769

Nicolas-Joseph Cugnot, who was born at Void, in Lorraine, on February 26, 1725 and died in Paris on October 10, 1804, built the first vehicle known to have been moved by mechanical power. His steam tractor, or *fardier*, was crude, it was slow, it often stopped, and it was apparently difficult to control, for the first version, probably designed in 1769, crashed into a wall; nevertheless it *was* self-propelled. The second version, built for the French Army a year later and preserved in Paris, is a milestone in the history of transport.

The ideas behind the *fardier* show great intelligence. The power-to-weight ratio is good, and it has a stout frame made of massive wood beams, resting on two rear wheels and a single front wheel that both drove and steered. A large fork supports the bucket-shaped copper fire-tube boiler, slung forward of the front wheel and complete with furnace and accessories. Un-

fortunately the boiler now to be seen in the Conservatoire may not be the original one.

The engine is the most interesting element. There are two parallel vertical cylinders that are cast in bronze with a 13-inch bore and a 12-inch stroke, giving a total displacement of about 50 liters. The direct motion of the connecting rods is transformed into rotary motion by a ratchet and pawl mechanism, one on each side of the front wheel.

An ingenious system of levers moves the taps that admit high-pressure steam to the single-acting cylinders. The tap on the boiler, with its long lever, controls the engine. The steering has a double reduction, first with 7-toothed and 21-toothed gears (3 to 1 reduction), and then with a 6-toothed pinion engaging with the circular rack that is mounted in one with the forecarriage, and has a ratio of at least 20 to 1. The wheel moves 15 degrees each way, but it is clear that the steering was too slow, even though the speed of the vehicle in tests proved to be little more than 2.2 miles per hour (3.5 kilometers). Moreover, the front wheel had to take the

These close-ups illustrate the massive character of the Fardier, *emphasized in the large photo overleaf. The chassis is built up of massive beams, but the mechanical elements are in excellent proportion. Left: Cugnot's ingenious rotating valve with rocker control.*

weight of the boiler and furnace, which made steering a major task.

Nevertheless the tractor proved itself capable of hauling a load of between 4 and 5 tons, but its demonstration at the Paris Arsenal was marred by the frequent necessity to refill the boiler, which was of inadequate capacity, and to generate more steam. Furthermore its large, unsprung wheels made it almost useless on any but smooth ground, so that its value as a means of towing guns—for which Cugnot had designed it—must have been limited.

Undoubtedly the *fardier* could have been improved with experience and encouragement, but unfortunately Cugnot got neither, for a change of Army policy made it redundant. Miraculously it survived the French Revolution to become a celebrated exhibit at the then recently opened Conservatoire des Arts et Métiers in 1801.

Panhard et Levassor M2E

1896

1,206 cc, producing about 4 horsepower at 800 rpm.

The engine is water-cooled with a pump driven by friction through a pulley in contact with the flywheel. Ignition is by the pioneer hot tube system and there is splash lubrication and a Maybach spray carburetor.

The leather-covered cone clutch could be controlled both by pedal and lever, and the 4-speed gearbox has a shaft with fixed gears and a countershaft with sliding gears, working on the famous *train baladeur* system, which is the basis of all conventional gearboxes.

Drive passed from the countershaft to a pair of bevel gears and finally to the differential. These bevels served both for forward motion and reverse, and thus the car had as many reverse speeds as forward. The differential is mounted on the chassis, and drive to the wheels is by side chains. Maximum speed was about 18.5 mph.

The frame is of wood, reinforced by steel plates, and it is interesting that the racing cars apparently had less reinforcement on the chassis in order to make them more flexible. Suspension is by semi-elliptic leaf springs at the front and by fully elliptic springs at the rear, and there are solid rubber tires on the wooden-spoked wheels.

Steering is by what the French called the "cow's tail," a plain lever or tiller instead of the wheel, which had yet to be popularized. There are two brakes, one worked by a lever that pressed two blocks against the rear wheels, and the other by a pedal-operated band brake on the solid drum of the countershaft.

Though somewhat rough and ready, this Panhard et Levassor, with its front-mounted, in-line engine, four-speed gearbox, and main control systems, contains all the basic elements of the conventional car.

In the earliest days of the motor car, Panhard et Levassor was the greatest of French makes, setting design trends and dominating the great town-to-town road races. In its twilight years it became simply Panhard, and it was finally absorbed by Citroën, who kept the name going until 1968.

The car in the Conservatoire is virtually a twin of the one with which 52-year-old Emile Levassor won a remarkable victory in the Paris–Bordeaux–Paris race in June 1895, covering the formidable distance of 732 miles in 48 hours, 48 minutes, driving the whole way himself, and averaging 15.00 mph.

The car, which can be seen today in Paris, has a Daimler Phénix engine, with its two cylinders disposed in line. The 80x120-mm bore and stroke give a displacement of

This legendary horseless carriage is given rather a saucy air by its fringed canopy and side curtains. The various engine lubricators can be seen in the picture on the right. Above, a rear wheel and chain drive in detail. Left, the neat folding step for rear seat access.

MUSEE DE LA VOITURE

Not many miles from Paris, in the midst of beautiful woodland, stands the palace of Compiègne, which houses the collection of horse-drawn and motor vehicles belonging to the French national museums. It is, in fact, a remote annex to the Louvre, dedicated to land transport. Because few authentic pieces have survived from earlier periods, the chronology of land transport has been reconstructed partly by means of models of pioneer vehicles exhibited in a series of halls.

Among the medieval examples is a simple farm cart, the ceremonial carriage in which Henry IV was assassinated, and the famous *char branlant,* which has the first attempt at a suspension system. Its body is hung from belts that are attached to a sort of chassis, clearly with the object of reducing the jarring from the appallingly rough roads of the time.

Representing a later period, there is the splendid pomp of the Louis XIV period coaches, fitted with glass and suspension systems of a pattern that was to endure until the close of the 19th century.

Unfortunately Compiègne has no royal coaches, for these were destroyed during the French Revolution. Among the more plebeian models, however, there are travelling *berlines*—handy, sturdy vehicles made for the highest speeds that a team of horses could manage on the roads of the period— and coaches of the English type. These differ from the French and Italian kinds in their sobriety, black being the prevailing color for finishing, and in the greater perfection of the mechanical parts such as suspension, axles, and wheels.

Alongside the coaches, French roads in the early 19th century also saw the appearance of the first bicycles, built by the German Baron von Drais around 1817 and called *Draisines* or *Draisiennes*. At Compiègne you can see an example of the first clumsy, pedal-less bicycle with wooden frame, and later machines with tubular steel frames and various pedal systems.

From the bicycle to the motor car, the step is a short one. The French contributed enormously to the invention and development of the automobile, thanks to the efforts of numerous inventors and research workers, from Cugnot to Lenoir, and of famous designers in the heroic period when the car moved out of its infancy.

Among the vehicles exhibited at Compiègne (some of which, unfortunately, have not been restored as well as one might desire) there are several interesting steam cars made by the Bollée family of Le Mans, as well as important electric and gas driven vehicles.

The Bollées, de Dion, and Serpollet are the major French exponents of steam traction, doomed to end in the 1920s. Kriéger is the best known name in electric cars, while Peugeot, Panhard et Levassor, and Renault all made vital contributions to the development of the gasoline-powered car.

The ground-floor rooms of the Compiègne museum are admirably suited to illustrating the evolution of wheeled transport through the years, from vehicles drawn by animals to the first motor cars. For all practical purposes the collection does not go beyond the end of the last century. Later vehicles belong to contemporary history and thus have been omitted from Compiègne, which stands as a museum in the classical sense of the word—an exhibition of relics of the past.

The Musée de la Voiture in the palace out in the woods lacks that immediate contact with reality that one finds at the Le Mans museum, where the roar of racing cars can be heard, or in the Paris Conservatoire des Arts et Métiers, where everything seems real. Yet the pilgrimage to Compiègne should not be neglected, for there you can see the first car to reach over 60 miles an hour, Jenatzy's unforgettable *Jamais Contente,* with other hallowed veterans keeping it mute company in the soft light that filters through the great windows of the palace.

Bollée La Mancelle

1878

The Bollée family of Le Mans has a strong claim to be among the earliest producers of horseless carriages, even if the chief interests of Amedée Bollée and his two sons, Léon and Amedée, lay in the manufacture of steam cars. These were such fine vehicles for their day that in numerous ways they anticipated the real automobile, and the fame of the *Obéissante,* the *Mancelle* and the *Rapide,* besides a number of others, was well earned—and not only for their delightful names.

The *Mancelle* is considered to be the Bollées' classic steam car creation. Apart from another small machine (the *Rapide*), the *Mancelle* was the most compact of their vehicles, for their main production centered around massive coaches and buses. Compared with the *Obéissante,* which weighed 4.9 tons (4,500 kilograms), the *Mancelle* at not much more than half that weight is a runabout, yet it could travel at 22 mph.

The frame was part wood, part metal, with the longitudinal members varying in shape, width and depth to accommodate the various components. The engine itself has two vertical in-line double-acting cylinders with the distributing valves in the middle, has an output of about 10 horsepower, and is mounted well to the front, overhanging the axle. A long drive shaft and an ingenious cone clutch take the drive to a differential and bevel gears, with short side chains and sprockets for the final drive—an anticipation of the so-called *système Panhard,* with front engine and rear drive. The wood-clad vertical boiler and water tanks are at the rear, with a little stand for the stoker (or *chauffeur*) that is protected by a canopy.

The driver sits at the front over the axle, behind a vertical steering column, while the steering wheel contains a smaller concentric wheel for controlling the engine. The handbrake acts by means of blocks on the rear wheels. There is seating capacity for six people.

Undoubtedly the most sensational element of this car is the forecarriage. In 1878, when others were still using the revolving forecarriage adapted from coach design, Bollée had *independent* wheel suspension with double transverse leaf springs (still used on some cars

On this small Bollée steam car the weight is well distributed, with the boiler at the rear, the power unit at the front, and the seats in between.

today), and applied one of the first compensated steering systems, based on a system of levers terminating in a toothed rack that engaged the keyed pinion on the steering column. The wheels of the *Mancelle* are of sturdy riveted iron, eloquent testimony to the poor road conditions of the time.

This Bolléé steam carriage was actually put into small-scale production at a price of 12,000 francs, and examples of it traveled as far as Vienna and Berlin.

De Dion Dogcart
1885

The company formed by the Count de Dion and the engineers Bouton and Trépardoux dates from 1881, when the young Parisian nobleman began to take an interest in things mechanical and, in particular, in the latest fashion in transport, the horseless carriage. In so doing, the Count ran the risk of being disinherited by his father, who took a far from favorable view of his son getting mixed up with "mechanics," but luckily this threat, which might have cost France one of its most brilliant industrialists, was not enforced.

The de Dion steam dogcart exhibited at Compiègne is one of the oldest known to exist, and is practically the first to be built in a small series rather than for experimental purposes. Although at the Compiègne museum it is dated 1885, this vehicle was probably built some years

MÊME ATTELÉS

It may not look like it, but the front of the de Dion is to the right in this view, for passengers on the rear seat faced backward. There can have been less risk of feeling the cold in the front seats, with the boiler under the occupants' noses! Note the curious wheel spokes.

later, since the de Dion concern initially experimented with steam tricycles, the first appearing in 1887.

Unusually, the first experimental four-wheeler de Dion had its steering wheels at the rear and its driving wheels at the front, but the dogcart at Compiègne reversed this order and assumed the more conventional layout. Its front-mounted boiler is of a special light pattern developed by Bouton and Trépardoux, and the engine has twin oscillating cylinders, a system patented by the company. It marked an important step forward in steam engine design, eliminating the crossheads and utilizing the oscillating movement of the cylinders to control the passage of steam.

For its day the de Dion steam dogcart was outstandingly light and fast (capable of about 19 mph or 30 kph), besides being one of the easiest to steer and handle. Even though its rugged appearance does not suggest very refined construction, what it lacked in elegance it made up for in quality.

The body of the example at Compiègne is a *dos à dos,* i.e., with two paired seats back to back. De Dion Bouton eventually abandoned steam for gasoline-powered cars, whereupon engineer Trépardoux left the company, but not before inventing the famous de Dion axle.

25

Jenatzy's Jamais Contente

1899

Even before the end of the 19th century, the rivalry between two intrepid racing drivers brought the automobile to the threshold of a speed of over 60 mph (100 kph). This was not the fastest absolute speed up to that time, as railway trains had traveled faster on selected sections of track, but many people believed that such a high speed on a motor car was impossible. If attained, they feared, it would cost the rash driver his life through asphyxiation.

Yet the Parisian Marquis de Chasseloup-Laubat and the Belgian Camille Jenatzy were able to disprove this theory as they dueled for the car speed record with rival electric cars. By March 1899 the Marquis had broken the record three times and Jenatzy twice, and now the Belgian resolved to take the record beyond reach by designing a completely new car.

This was the *Jamais Contente* (Never Satisfied), with a bullet-shaped body in light alloy set high on an un-

Judging from its appearance, Jamais Contente *might have been built in about 1910 and not 1899. Below, the little central leaf spring is not part of the suspension but a flexible link for the steering. Above: from where Jenatzy sat the controls look fairly simple—but at 65 mph. . . .*

streamlined chassis, and two battery-driven electric motors, each capable of over 1,000 rpm and geared down to drive the rear wheels. The streamlined body was filled with batteries, and considering the weight of the car and its times through the standing-start kilometer and the following kilometer, which counted for the record, its maximum power can be calculated at about 12 horsepower per motor.

This power could only be kept up for the short time of the record run, as the motors were heavily "overvolted" and the batteries underwent a violent discharge. On April 29, 1899 Jenatzy broke the land speed record in *Jamais Contente* at a speed of 65.80 mph (105.9 kph), a figure that stood unbroken for three years.

Preserved today in the museum at Compiègne, Jenatzy's famous car is remarkable for the modern appearance of its 25.5-inch-diameter Michelin pneumatic tires, for its double rear semi-elliptic springs, and its strange mixture of antiquity and modern streamlining. The driver sat up high in the wind, steering his mount by a handlebar and adjusting the speed by the series and parallel combination of the two motors and the batteries.

The brakes are on the rear wheels, operated by a lever and steel cable device that balances the braking force on the two wheels.

Jamais Contente was the world's first car built specially to break a speed record, and in exceeding 60 mph back in 1899 it also disproved the old belief that man would die for want of air at such a velocity!

MUSEE DE L'AUTOMOBILE

In the heart of the Sarthe district, outside the ancient town of Le Mans, lies the circuit where every June the Le Mans 24-Hour Race is fought out. It is one of the most famous car races in the world. It is not, however, one of the oldest in motoring history. The first edition of the race did not take place until 1923, when there was mounting interest in sporting cars and a keen desire to see how long they could withstand racing at high speed on give-and-take French roads, both by day and by night.

Since that first very successful race, the Grand Prix d'Endurance has become an annual classic and a great tradition in French motor sport, with a character all its own. Among its many attractions is the famous *village* of amusements clustered around the pit area, and an interesting addition there in recent years is the *Musée de l'Automobile*.

This important museum is the concrete expression of the enthusiasm of M. Bernard de Lassée who, besides making over his own private collection of cars, has dedicated a great deal of time and experience to the museum's creation. The museum is composed of two main buildings. The one that also serves as the entrance is made

LE MANS

largely of glass, and thus is flooded with light, while the second is an extended structure in which artificial lighting has to be used.

The many racing, sports, and touring cars exhibited are tastefully displayed and are protected by low scaffolding. The value of the collection is enhanced by many vehicles of great historical value, including the armored Mercedes-Benz used by Hitler and the Socéma-Gregoire, France's first gas turbine car, built in 1952.

Appropriately, there are also cars that have taken part in the Le Mans 24-Hour Race; but perhaps the finest part of the collection is the veteran section, grouped in the entrance hall, which includes pioneer vehicles built at Le Mans by the illustrious Bollée family who originated in this town and called one of their most famous steam cars *La Mancelle*. There are also very early examples of Benz, Panhard et Levassor, Renault, and Delahaye cars, two de Dion steamers, and the curious propeller-driven Marcel-Leyat device of 1920.

The museum is, of course, a considerable attraction to visitors during all races run on the circuit. Besides the 24-Hour Race, lesser events are staged on the shorter inner

course, named after Bugatti, and also important motorcycle races. The museum differs from many others in containing modern as well as old exhibits, and, in fact, the apron in front of the entrance dedicated to Pininfarina, the famous Turin coachbuilder whose work has had such a great influence on the style of modern motor cars.

The museum engages in various motoring activities, M. de Lassée often taking his own superb 1912 sports SPA car off its stand to drive it in Continental veteran car rallies. Cars are also loaned from other collections for special occasions. For example, on the occasion of the 60th anniversary of the Grand Prix de l'Automobile Club de France, the FIAT with which Nazzaro won the 1907 race, normally exhibited at the Biscaretti museum in Turin, was displayed at Le Mans during the period of the 24-Hour Race.

It is interesting to note that this museum has an offshoot at Lourdes, where the 60 cars include a rare early Panhard 1929 record-breaking car of the same make, and a 1937 Le Mans Simca. The two museums exchange cars in order to vary their respective exhibits.

Delahaye Break

1896

This is a rare surviving participant from the legendary 1896 Paris–Marseilles–Paris road race, one of the most grueling of all the pioneer motoring events, in which the competitors were assailed by a tremendous storm and faced hazards including trees uprooted and fallen across the road, hurricane-force winds, drenching rain, and floods. Two Delahayes competed, finishing seventh and tenth. During the race, the crew of one was obliged en route to saw their way through a tree brought down by the storm and blocking the road.

It is probable that the Delahaye at the Le Mans museum was built the year before the race; certainly it follows the layout of the very earliest cars, which bore a marked resemblance to horse-drawn carriages. Yet there are several ingenious mechanical details.

The engine is a large, parallel, twin-cylinder unit, mounted horizontally at the rear, and water-cooled. Bore and stroke are 110x140 mm, giving a total displacement of 2,661 cc. Various sources state the power to be 6 or 8 horsepower at 700 rpm, but everything points to the effective power being at least 8 horsepower, since this Delahaye could reach 18.5 mph (30 kph) while carrying four substantial people.

Automatic inlet valves are used, as was normal practice then, while the exhaust valves are cam-operated. Gravity lubrication is by the usual drip-feed oilers; ignition is electric, by coil and condensers, which is advanced for the time; and cooling is by a centrifugal pump and tubular radiator. The throws of the crankshaft are at 180 degrees, making for somewhat harsh running at low speeds.

The transmission is interesting: the engine turns a shaft with three belt pulleys, one of which is free and provides neutral. By shifting the belt onto one or the other driving pulleys, two forward ratios are obtained. Reverse and a lower gear are, on the other hand, obtained with a change lever connected to the pulley shaft. Final drive is by chain.

The Delahaye has a brazed tubular frame with leaf spring suspension all around, fully elliptic at the front, and semi-elliptic at the rear. The steering is by a curious vertical handlebar (the gear controls are also on the steering column), with reduction and transmission of motion by means of a chain to a lever operating the wheels. These have wooden spokes and solid tires, although as run in the 1896 Paris–Marseilles–Paris the Delahayes were fitted with early pneumatics all around.

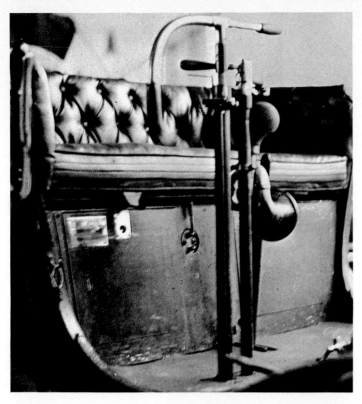

These three photographs show many of the most interesting details of the Delahaye Break. Above, the rear axle with exposed connecting rods and the pulley system for changing gear. Left, the controls with the odd, asymmetrical tiller curving down to one side. Below, the tubular radiator and the chain steering system.

Panhard et Levassor B1

1898

This car is certainly one of the first touring Panhard et Levassors fitted with a four-cylinder engine, which had previously only been tried out on racing cars. Like all early cars of this make, it has an engine built under a Daimler license, with two blocks of two cylinders, like two Phénix units mounted, in line, in a single crankcase. The cylinder dimensions are 80-mm bore and 120-mm stroke, giving a total engine capacity of 2,412 cc and a power output of 12 horsepower at less than 1,000 rpm.

Engine speed adjustment is by a centrifugal regulator driven by the camshaft, with lever and pedal control. The inlet valves are automatic and the exhausts mechanical; on the racing cars *bruleur* (platinum tube) ignition was still used. This car has a Bosch high-tension magneto. Cooling is by water with pump and a tubular radiator. The clutch is of the leather-covered cone type, and there are four forward speeds and reverse with two control levers, one of which engages reverse only. Final drive is by chain.

Braking is by a footbrake on the transmission and handbrake with bands wrapping around drums on the rear wheels (i.e., external contracting). Both brake controls disengage the clutch before slowing the car, for the braking power of the engine had not been appreciated in 1898. The chassis is straight throughout its length, with outriggers carrying semi-elliptic leaf spring suspension for both axles. The wooden-spoked wheels mount 875x105 tires at the front and 920x120 at the rear.

The body is made of aluminum, which is a novelty for a touring car of that period. It is upholstered with the characteristic buttoned leather, while at the back there is a trunk made of basket work, which was handy for storing an umbrella in case of rain. The hood is

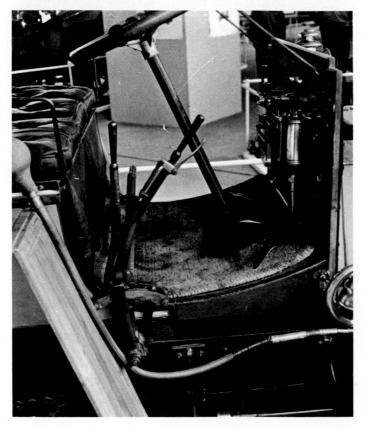

The dashboard of this Panhard is entirely taken up by pumps and lubricators (left). The sprag brake can be seen beside the right-hand rear wheel (right). Note the great mass of the tubular radiator, and the single front headlamp.

distinguished by the characteristic polished brass bevelling of the early Panhards.

An interesting control detail is the application of two hand levers on the spokes of the steering wheel, one for controlling the engine, the other for the "sprag" brake, which was used on hills to avoid running back and to spare the normal brakes, which were fairly efficient in the forward direction, but rather delicate when the car ran back. Weight of the Panhard type B1 was about 1770 lb, and it reached a maximum speed just over 30 mph.

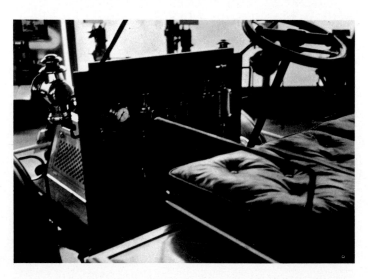

Bollée Limousine

1901

The unusual shape of this Bollée limousine, and the fact that the makers were pioneers of steam transport, often led to it being mistaken for a steam car. The horizontal twin-cylinder engine and the two tubular radiators, one each side of the hood, can be seen (right and below). With a weight of over 3920 pounds, the car is very strong.

The Bollées, father and sons, of Le Mans, are famed for their steam coaches, but when they, too, engaged in the production of internal combustion-engined cars, they made some fine specimens, including this imposing *limousine de ville* by the Amédée brothers in 1901, with two outside front seats and internal accommodation for six people on the two seats.

The short, high body was manufactured by Carrosserie Dauploy and epitomizes the transitory stage of development between the first horseless carriages and the true automobile. This limousine remains today in a perfect state of repair.

The engine is a horizontal parallel twin, notable for employing much aluminum in its construction. Diameter of each cylinder is 110 mm, and stroke 160 mm, giving a total displacement of 3,041 cc. The power from the engine is about 9–10 horsepower at less than 1,000 rpm. There are automatic inlet valves and exhaust valves driven by a single tappet, which opens the two valves in turn. Fuel feed is by Bollée automatic carburetor—the first in the world to have a submerged jet.

Ignition was originally by platinum tubes and *bruleur*, but a battery and coil system was adapted to this particular car in 1907. One of the performance figures that was recorded was a fuel consumption of 12 liters per 100 km, or approximately 20 miles per gallon. Cooling was a pioneer example of the closed-circuit type, with two condensers shaped like finned towers placed one on each side of the distinctive tapered hood.

Transmission is through a cone clutch and a four-speed gearbox (with the control lever on the steering column), and final drive is by side chains. The chassis has U-section steel side members and ample cross-bracing—an advanced concept for 1901. Suspension is by fully elliptic leaf springs at the front and by semi-elliptic springs at the rear. The wooden-spoked wheels mount 900x90 tires at the front and 920x120 at the rear. The wheelbase is remarkably short for such a large car, being only 78 inches, while the track measures about 52 inches.

The example preserved at Le Mans has three imposing brass acetylene headlamps, with a centralized plant for the gas.

In general, this Bollée is a car whose advanced mechanical design lies concealed beneath the ornate carriage styling typical of that period in car evolution.

Darracq Type N

1901

Alexandre Darracq came into the motor industry via bicycles and motorcycles, founding the Gladiator, Millet, and Perfecta concerns prior to creating the Darracq make before the end of the 19th century. His first serious car was the Leon-Bollée tourer built under license as the Darracq-Bollée, but in 1900 he produced the first Darracq tourer, which included a 785-cc single-cylinder engine.

The 1901 Type N exhibited at Le Mans is an intermediate stage between that 1900 tourer and later, larger Darracqs. Its front-mounted, single-cylinder engine is water-cooled, with a tubular radiator of distinctive rectangular shape, notably modern for the time. The cylinder dimensions are 90x100 mm, giving an engine capacity of 636 cc: that is to say, smaller than the 1900 unit but higher powered at about 8–9 horsepower

at 1,500 rpm, thanks to the introduction of mechanically operated inlet valves. On the earlier model these were automatically operated by suction.

The Type N Darracq has high-tension ignition, while lubrication is by drip-feed oilers. A leather-covered cone clutch is housed in the flywheel, and the three-speed gearbox is separate from the engine. The gear lever is on the steering column, together with the other control levers for the engine. The final drive is by drive shaft, for Darracq, like Renault, stood out from the mass of earlier designers in never using chain drive.

The front axle is tubular, suspended by semi-elliptic leaf springs; this type of spring is also used at the rear, in conjunction with a third spring, mounted transversely across the extreme rear of the steel chassis. Wooden-spoked artillery-type wheels carry 710x90 tires all around. The weight of the car is about 600 kg (roughly 1320 pounds), and with a maximum speed of over 31 mph (50 kph), effective brakes and reliable performance, the Type N Darracq was a popular little car in its day.

The example at the Le Mans museum has an open four-seater body with access to the rear seats by a door in the back panel opening rearward, with a small hung step to help the passengers climb in. The real significance of this car is that it was one of the world's first quantity-production models, marketed at a modest price.

The main controls of the Type N Darracq are all on the steering column (far right). The gear lever is the thick one under the wheel; there is a spark advance, a hand accelerator, and a mixture control.

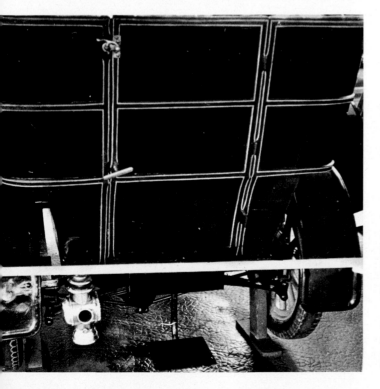

Le Zèbre Type A

1909

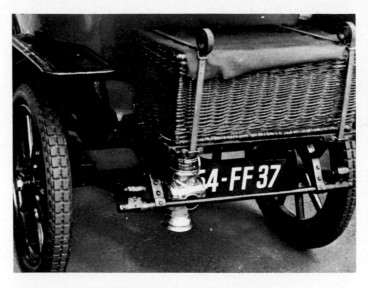

The Le Zèbre Type A, which was produced from 1909 to 1914, might well be described as one of the world's first "personal" cars, built for individual transport for one or at most two persons, at a reasonable price. The designer was Jules Salomon, who succeeded in producing a miniature car that could be manufactured economically yet was in many ways similar to a large one. It was apparently very popular with people whose work enabled them to appreciate its qualities, such as doctors, priests, and commercial travelers.

In fact, although the Type A has a single-cylinder engine, it is placed at the front under a hood with lines following the fashion of the period, making the car seem larger than it really is. This engine has side valves, and the cylinder dimensions are 86x106-mm bore and stroke, giving 630 cc total displacement. The maxi-

mum power developed is about 6 horsepower.

Cooling is by water and a handsome brass radiator, and high-tension ignition by Bosch magneto. The carburetor is gravity-fed from a fuel tank mounted behind the tire wall, which is above and behind the engine, while lubrication is by the "total loss" system. The oil tank also resides conveniently behind the firewall. The gearbox has only two forward speeds and reverse, and drive to the rear axle is by propeller shaft, enhancing the impression the Le Zèbre gives of being a large car in miniature.

The frame consists of pressed-steel side members and tubular cross-bracing, the whole bolted and riveted together. Suspension of both axles is by semi-elliptic leaf springs; 26x3-inch tires are mounted on wooden-spoked wheels, and the fenders are light but adequate.

A spartan runabout must surely have been the aim of the Le Zèbre designer. Note the driving seat completely shorn of accessories or instruments, and the few controls. The large tank at the driver's feet is for gas.

This little car has a wheelbase of only 71 inches and is exceptionally light for the period, weighing no more than 700 pounds. It had a maximum speed of close to 30 mph. It was sold at a very low basic price, with essentials such as a sturdy windshield, an effective hood, head and tail lamps, and other equipment selling as "optional extras." One such example is the wicker basket that can be seen on the car at Le Mans; mounted at the rear, this was very useful, particularly for commercial travelers, and was a true precursor of the trunk of modern times.

An indication of Salomon's modern conception is provided by the controls; these are as simple as possible, with all levers mounted inside the car at a time when it was still fashionable to place them outside.

Hurtu Type X

1910

It was only after many years of activity, producing varied metal goods from sewing machines to bicycles, that the French firm of Hurtu began making motor cars. They started out in this field by building tourers for Bollée, then went on to launch their own models, initially based on the German belt-drive Benz.

Thanks to the experience they acquired, the cars Hurtu subsequently produced were reliable even if not particularly inspiring in appearance with their dashboard radiators, as pioneered by Renault several years before. On the other hand, it is interesting to note that this French light car of pre-World War I days has an in-line, four-cylinder sleeveless engine with side-by-side valves and adequate capacity to ensure regularity in running, and also the advanced feature for the day of unit construction of the engine and gearbox.

Dimensions of the four cylinders are 70-mm bore and 100-mm stroke giving a total displacement of 1,539 cc. The power recorded in the literature of the day is "7 horsepower," which is French fiscal horsepower equal to about 10 horsepower in the English Royal Automobile Club rating, or approximately 17 horsepower. Maximum speed of the car was around 28 mph (45 kph).

The Hurtu 4X is water-cooled with thermosiphon circulation and has high-tension ignition and a vertical barrel-type carburetor. There is a cone clutch and three forward speeds and reverse. The gear lever and handbrake lever are externally mounted. The brakes act on the rear wheels in the classic manner—i.e., the handbrake on the wheels and the footbrake on the drive train.

The chassis and suspension follow the conventions of the period; the former is of pressed steel, while the latter employ semi-elliptic leaf springs at the front and three-quarter elliptic leaf springs at the rear. Final drive

is by propeller shaft, and the wood-spoked wheels carry 710x90 tires.

Considering that the Hurtu 4X to be seen at the Le Mans museum is only a two-seater, the wheelbase seems unusually long at 94 inches, making the tail, which lacks a jump seat, appear out of proportion. It is probable, however, that one standard wheelbase model served for all types of bodywork offered by the firm of Hurtu.

This was another popular French runabout. The mascot on the radiator cap is a bulldog's head. Note external handbrake and gear lever, not too accessible with the hood sticks in the way. Weight of the Hurtu 4X was about 1370 pounds, and it could attain 28 mph. Note (top right) the excessive length of the trunk, which has no jump seat.

$\mathcal{SPA}\ 25hp$

1912

This two-seater sports car on a 1912 25-horsepower SPA chassis has an extremely elegant body and anticipates the graceful open "Spyder" bodies that graced many Italian sports chassis in the late 1920s and early 1930s. The bodywork was specially built, it is believed, in 1913, and Rudge-Whitworth wire wheels with identical 820x120 tires all around were fitted instead of the standard wooden-spoked wheels with smaller front

tires. The car is the property of M. Bernard de Lassée, Director of the Le Mans museum.

Its engine is a sleeveless, in-line four-cylinder with 100x140-mm bore and stroke (4,398 cc), and the factory specification indicates a maximum power of 30 horsepower at 1,200–1,500 rpm, and a maximum speed of around 68 mph (110 kph). A single-choke carburetor and side-by-side valves are used, the camshaft is in the crankcase, ignition is by high-tension magneto, and the cooling is by centrifugal pump, fan, and honeycomb radiator.

Transmission is through a multi-plate clutch, a gearbox with four speeds and reverse, and shaft final drive to a rigid rear axle. The chassis has channel steel side members with cross-bracing, and suspension is by semi-elliptic leaf springs at the front, and three-quarter elliptics at the back. Braking is on the rear wheels, worked by the handbrake lever, and on the transmission, just behind the gearbox, worked by the footbrake.

The SPA is thus of conventional design beneath that striking "torpedo" bodywork, but it is beautifully engineered and finished to the SPA concern's high manufacturing standards. The gear and handbrake levers are set outside the car, and the two seats are slightly staggered to provide greater comfort in the rather narrow body. The long sweeping fenders, their front and rear

This is a sports version of the production 25-horsepower SPA, fitted with a special two-seater body. A large clock stands out on the dashboard, and the spark and carburetion controls are on the steering wheel. The car belongs to the director of Le Mans museum, Bernard de Lassée.

sections almost a replica of each other, are divided by a tiny runningboard.

The big main headlamps are acetylene, with the gas generator on the right-hand runningboard; there are also two small oil lamps. Bernard de Lassée has driven this car with notable success in many Continental historic car rallies, *concours d'élégance,* and so forth. The initials SPA denote Societa Piemontese Automobili—the full name of the manufacturers—who also built aircraft and marine engines until they were absorbed by FIAT in the 1920s.

Chenard-Walcker Tank

1925

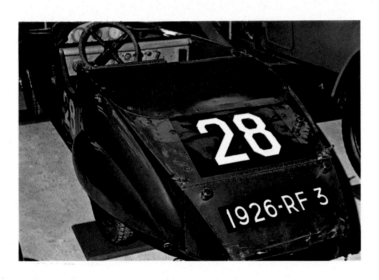

The dashboard of this unusual little French car has a stark, aeronautical purpose about it. The aerodynamic bodywork is formed in aluminum sheet and effectively shrouds the rear wheels. This roadster was highly successful in sports car racing.

This little car, with its curious aerodynamic body—which makes it look more like a tank than anything—is, in fact, one of the most successful ever produced by the French Chenard-Walcker factory. Their 3-liter cars had done very well in the first edition of the Le Mans 24 Hour Race in 1923, coming in first and second, but two years later they neglected their bigger-engined machines to present this radically new racing model with its small, 66x80-mm four-cylinder engine, having a total displacement of only 1,094 cc. It performed excellently, winning the 1,100 cc class of the 1925 Le Mans 24-Hour Race, and scored many significant victories subsequently.

The engine of the Tank Chenard has overhead valves, water cooling, single carburetor, magneto ignition, and pressure lubrication. One version had a Cozette vane-type supercharger, which raised its maximum speed from the 94.5 mph (152 kph) of the car illustrated here to a remarkable 106.9 mph (172 kph).

Mechanically, the remainder of the car is fairly conventional, with four-speed gearbox, single dry-plate clutch, live rear axle, and all around semi-elliptic springing. Hydraulic dampers were advanced equipment for the time; the frame is of pressed steel channel section, well braced for rigidity, and drum brakes with mechanical operation are fitted to all four wheels.

By far the most interesting part of the car is its beetle-shaped body, formed in aluminum sheet; there are large flat surfaces to simplify construction, but also, perhaps, because it was believed they would make it more efficient aerodynamically.

Certainly the shape of the Tank must have contributed to its performance, for the speeds it attained were remarkably high considering the small engine. No windshield was used in its years of racing, but a cowling over the steering wheel served to deflect wind from the driver's face. The Rudge-Whitworth wire wheels carried discs to improve the streamlining further, and the rear wheels were well covered by fairings.

The success of the little Chenard was a lesson in streamlining, unfortunately little heeded at the time.

Salmson Sports

1927

The Salmson firm of Billancourt, Paris, originally engaged in the manufacture of airplane engines, branched out into the production of cyclecars, made under license from the British GN Company, and then naturally moved onto roadsters. These sold extremely well in the 1920s, thanks partly to their brilliant racing successes at Le Mans, Brooklands, Boulogne and other circuits, but also because of their liveliness and excellent performance on the road, and their modest price. The Salmson was, indeed, the most popular French sports car of all in the period between the two world wars, playing a vital part in spreading the sports car movement throughout Europe.

The 1927 version at the Le Mans museum has the characteristic Salmson rakish wings and pointed tail,

and the radiator with the distinctive diagonals. It has a four-cylinder, in-line engine with a 62x90-mm bore and stroke, giving 1,087 cc and a power output of about 33 horsepower at 3,800 rpm. With the very modest road weight of under 1120 pounds, the Salmson had a high power/weight ratio and a correspondingly lively performance, with a maximum speed of 75 mph.

On the earlier touring versions of the Salmson roadster a pushrod overhead valve engine was used, but the Sport model as seen at the Le Mans museum has twin overhead camshafts. A Cozette compressor is fitted to the more potent Grand Prix Special and San Sebastian models, in place of the normal single Solex 30-mm carburetor and magneto ignition.

A three-speed gearbox was normally fitted to road models, but four speeds were available as an optional extra. A single dry-plate clutch is used, and final drive is by propeller shaft, worm gear, and pinion. No differential is fitted, contributing to the Salmson's light weight, and its brisk but sometimes crablike cornering. The chassis has shallow side members, and springing is by semi-elliptics at the front and quarter-elliptics at the rear. Outstanding on such a light car are the Perrot mechanical brakes—among the best of their time—on all four wheels. These are of Rudge-Whitworth wire type with "knock-off" quick-release hubcaps, and carry 27x4-inch tires, which add to the Salmson's spidery but attractive appearance.

The Salmson was one of the fine little French racing cars in the 1,100-cc class that made history in the 1920s. Its specification is orthodox, and its high performance was due to lightness and an efficient engine.

45

MUSÉE FRANÇAISE DE L'AUTOMOBILE HENRI MALARTRE

On the river Saône at Rochetaillée, not far from the city of Lyons, stands an ancient château, the feudal residence in the Middle Ages of the *Seigneurs* de Villars. It was ceded to the clergy of Lyons in the 11th century, was burned by the Huguenots in 1562, restored, fell into decay; later it was restored to its former beauty. Today the Château de Rochetaillée houses a remarkable collection of truly historic cars, making it one of the finest museums in France.

M. Henri Malartre, the son of a metallurgical industrialist, followed firmly in his father's footsteps until by chance his interest in old cars was aroused. One of the many activities of the Malartre firm was the collection of foundry scrap and vehicle parts, and every day several cars would be towed to the works to be demolished. Around 1929, an 1895 Rochet-Schneider appeared —a relic of a bygone age.

Malartre was intrigued by the old car, and before handing it over to his workmen, he decided to see if it was still in working order. After a few attempts, the engine coughed to life, and something in that veteran vehicle spoke to Malartre, convincing him that old cars should not be scrapped but revered, preserved, and, whenever possible, put into running order.

Of course, not every car brought to the Malartre yard for scrapping was worth sav-

ROCHETAILLEE

ing, but every now and then in the midst of the old iron appeared a rare piece, standing out like a diamond in the mud. The search at first was slow, and two years passed between Malartre's first rescue of a historic car and his second. During the decade before World War II, he managed to collect only seventeen.

After the war the cause was taken up again with much enthusiasm; those cars already restored and in running order were sent to meetings, or shown on premises belonging to the collector, but the right place for exhibiting them had yet to be found. Then the Château de Rochetaillée became available and was chosen by Henri Malartre to inaugurate his museum in 1960.

For car-loving visitors Rochetaillée offers a magnificent spectacle. The cars are artistically displayed in the various rooms according to their age and type. Almost 200 vehicles—cars, motorcycles, fire engines, and bicycles—innumerable models, historic posters, accessories, and miscellanea are on show, ranging from pre-gasoline steam cars to that old Rochet-Schneider first rescued by M. Malartre, through the rich chapters of automobile history to recent creations of importance.

There are many racing cars, shown in a special modern hall, including examples of Lago-Talbot, Rolland-Pilain, Gordini, Bugatti, Ferrari, and Osca, and other significant cars such as the mid-engined coupe built by J-P Wimille in 1948 and a prototype of the 2CV Citroën.

There are also interesting motorcycles, while the collection of components forms a veritable encyclopedia of motor engineering. There is a rudimentary sprag brake to prevent a car from running backward on a hill, which is simply a spike lowered at the rear; there are the finest twin-barrel carburetors, mounted on engines from early in the century, such as the F.N. and the Gladiator; there are opposed piston engines, dry-sump lubrication systems, and representatives of many types of ignition.

Among the rich selection of accessories are oil, acetylene, and early electric lamps, while one car, a 1904 Panhard, has a small compressor driven by the engine for inflating the tires. The same car has acetylene headlamps with a small, manually controlled dimmer in the form of a screen, which drops down between the flame and the mirror. A thousand and one fascinating gadgets of days gone by are to be viewed, saved by the man who could have destroyed them but decided not to.

Nor do the cars stand on show alone. The Rochetaillée vehicles are actively used in veteran vintage rallies—the château often is a starting point for such events.

Scotte Steam Wagonette

1892

Unlike most steam-engined vehicles of its day, the Scotte steam wagonette, built in 1892, has the whole engine unit at the front, suggesting an early version of the British Sentinel wagon. The boiler, however, is set to one side, and the twin-cylinder vertical engine is mounted transversely to the offside of the boiler. The

Were it not for the rare example preserved at Rochetaillée, this make, once well known, would be forgotten today. This Scotte steam car is agleam with polished copper piping and brass controls, wheel hubs, etc. The steering wheel looks like a cross between a bicycle wheel and a ship's tiller with its internal spokes and four external wooden handles.

vehicle in the Rochetaillée museum is a splendid and unique example of an early French steam road carriage, superbly restored to working order for Henry Malartre's museum.

It is reported that the coal-fired Field-type vertical boiler took rather a long time to get up steam—more than half an hour, in fact—but that once a head was built up it performed well. The engine and boiler were built to work at a pressure of eight atmospheres, so it is to be assumed (although definite figures are lacking) that the power available was about 10 horsepower.

Drive to the rear axle is through a countershaft and a belt final drive. Later Scotte steamers used chain transmission and a transposed engine/boiler layout. The water tank is mounted on the roof of the vehicle; the system did not employ a condenser. Speed adjustment

and reverse are obtained by a regulator controlling the position of the valves in the valve chest, and maximum speed was a trundling 7.5 mph (12 kph).

The chassis of the Scotte is a framework of U-shaped iron sections bolted together. The front axle is suspended on semi-elliptic leaf springs, while at the rear there are two longitudinal semi-elliptic leaf springs and a third, transverse, leaf spring mounted centrally beneath the rear chassis cross member. The wheels are wooden-spoked with iron tires, very like cart wheels.

The overall length of the wagonette is little more than 108 inches, and it weighs roughly two tons (1,835 kg). The passenger compartment has only two seats, but later models were simply extended rearward by two yards or so to accommodate up to twelve people.

De Dion-Bouton Doctor's Coupe

1900

This delightful little car is a variation of a model that earned wide renown in the early days of motoring. The little rear-engined single-cylinder de Dion-Bouton was, in fact, built in thousands around the turn of the century. The type most commonly known is the four-seater "*vis à vis*" with open body, whereas the car in the Rochetaillée museum is a closed two-seater. This particular model was very popular with the medical profession, thanks to the shelter it offered from wind, rain, and cold, hence the name Doctor's Coupe.

Mechanically the de Dion tourer is an outstanding example of practical simplicity and technical perfection. Many versions of the engine were built, with different displacements and power. This one has the 4.5 horsepower engine, with an 84x90-mm bore and stroke, and a capacity of 499 cc. The effective power is produced at about 1,500 rpm, and the inlet valve is automatically operated, and is located above the exhaust valve.

The engine is water-cooled, with the radiator hung low at the front; high-tension ignition is used, and the carburetor was manufactured by de Dion itself. A separate gearbox consists of a two-speed constant mesh gear and an ingenious system of expanding clutches, allowing either of the two gears or neutral to be engaged. Gear changing is carried out by means of a lever on the steering column in front of the driver and is extremely simple. Instead of a steering wheel, there is a kind of handlebar arrangement.

The chassis is made of brazed steel tubes, and suspension is by semi-elliptic leaves at the front. At the rear is the famous de Dion axle, invented by Bouton's brother-in-law Trépardoux, when he was working on their steam cars. This axle separates the wheels from the fixed differential housing, the drive shafts being universally jointed, and was an enormous improvement on chain drive.

The Doctor's Coupe is rather heavy, weighing 500 kg (1100 pounds) as compared with the 770 pounds (350 kg) of the normal version. This is due to the

This dainty little coupe could travel at about 24 mph. The bowler-hatted, dust-coated figure in the picture on the wall is Georges Bouton, faithful business partner to the Count de Dion.

heavier wooden wheels with 710x90 tires, and to the closed body with a larger glass area. The extra weight must have detracted from its performance, which on the standard, open four-seater models included a maximum speed of around 24 mph. The makers were de Dion, Douton, et Cie., of Puteaux, Paris.

This little three-wheeler is a curiosity of the Rochetaillée museum. With two electric motors it could travel at 12.5 mph for about 2 hours.

Mildé Electric Car

1900

The name of Charles Mildé is nowadays virtually forgotten, but from the end of the 19th century until 1909, his factory in the Rue Desrenaudes in Paris turned out excellent motor cars and commercial vehicles powered by electricity. Mildé also built some "gasoline electrics," with gasoline engines driving generators, which in turn drove electric motors.

The 1900 three-wheeler at the Le Mans museum is perfectly preserved and typifies the sound, sturdy Mildé approach to design. As far as the body is concerned, it is little more than a seat for two people, mounted on three wheels, but the mechanism is of considerable interest.

The batteries are placed under the seat, and there are two electric motors, one for each of the rear driving wheels. They are geared down through a small pinion on the motor and a large, internally geared crown wheel applied directly to the wheel. The whole electrical unit forms part of the rear axle, suspended on leaf springs. The motors are of the composite band type, and from a combination of the two in series and parallel, a large number of forward speeds and reverse can be obtained, with the car running very sweetly.

The frame is a tubular structure with some semblance to a modern space frame. The steering is through a wheel, a stout vertical column, and a complex arrangement of wheels and chains that turn the front wheel on rollers running in fixed circular guides—a sound but heavy process. The wheelbase between the rear axle and the single front wheel is 61 inches and the rear track is 45.5 inches. The rear tires have to support a concentration of weight on the axle, and measure 880x120, but these are possibly not as originally fitted.

The weight of the Mildé tricar is given as 320 kg (over 700 pounds), and in view of the scanty capacity of the batteries, its range cannot have been more than 20–25 miles, at a maximum speed of 12.5 mph. Certainly the small lantern above the front wheel does not suggest long-distance driving!

Peugeot Double Phaeton

1903

The ancient house of Peugeot produced so many car models in their early days, all with different characteristics and performance, that until the manufacturers published a catalog in the late 1960s, listing all their production from the very first model up to 1968, it was very difficult to trace or recognize them all.

The 1903 3.6-liter double phaeton is listed on page 23 of the first volume of the Peugeot catalog as having the following characteristics: four-cylinder, in-line side valve engine in two blocks of two cylinders, cooled by pump, fan, and honeycomb radiator. The 105x105-mm bore and stroke make it one of the "square" engines of the period, and total displacement is a substantial 3,635 cc. The engine has pressure lubrication and magneto ignition. The fiscal power is 18 CV, and the effective power cannot have been much greater at the 1,200 maximum rpm.

There is a cone clutch, and the gearbox-differential group is separate from the engine and mounted halfway along the chassis, as was general practice in those days of mixed transmissions. The box has four forward speeds and reverse, with an orthodox differential and chain drive to the rear wheels. The gear lever is set on the right-hand side on a single support together with the handbrake, which acts on the drums of the rear wheels. The footbrake works on the transmission.

Chassis and suspension follow convention, with pressed-steel side members and rigid axles on semi-elliptic leaf springs at front and rear. The wooden-spoked artillery wheels are fitted with 910x120 tires all around. Ahead of the driver is a wooden dashboard, and the engine controls are on the steering column.

Wheelbase of the Peugeot is a seemingly modest 77 inches, but in assessing its size, account must be taken of the large diameter wheels. The track, both front and rear, measures 58 inches. A feature of the 3.6-liter Peugeot was its extremely precise worm-and-nut steering, and the car was well spoken of in its time for quality of manufacture, comfort, and performance. It had a maximum speed of close to 50 mph (80 kph), but with no windshield this can only have been enjoyable in warm, dry weather, although even then there was the dust problem caused by unpaved roads.

In 1903, when this car was built, Peugeot was already a well-known make. The sweep of the fenders was designed to deflect the stream of air, and thus the dust, away from the car and its high-perched occupants. With a 3.6-liter engine it could attain almost 50 mph.

Corre Tonneau

1904

There has been a certain amount of confusion about the Corre make, as there was more than one firm of this name. Jean Corre, an ex-racing cyclist, founded the original company in Paris in 1901, then left it to found another in 1908. From that time the cars produced by the first company were called Corre-La Licorne (meaning Unicorn, which was the trademark) to distinguish them from the models of the second firm.

The 1904 Corre "tonneau" model to be seen at Le Mans was produced by the original factory. It has an Aster front-mounted, four-cylinder engine, with its cylinders cast in two blocks of two. It is water-cooled and has side valves. Aster engines had an excellent reputation and were used by many firms in this period.

The most interesting feature of this car is its flexible wheels, designed to dispense with the need for pneumatic tires. Unusual, too, are the lateral radiators. Weight is over 2660 pounds, and speed about 40 mph.

Engine dimensions are 100x140 mm for a 4,398-cc displacement and a French fiscal power of 25 CV. Ignition is by high-tension magneto, fuel feed by carburetor, and there is a mixed system of lubrication. The cooling system includes two radiators set at the sides of the Renault-like hood, and, therefore, only partially exposed to the air, so that adequate cooling was obtained thanks only to their size.

But undoubtedly the feature of outstanding interest on this particular car is that it is one of the few cars with flexible wheels that has been preserved. Wheels of this kind, which have been the dream of countless inventors, even in our time, are designed with the aim of eliminating the need for tires, relying instead on the flexibility of the wheels themselves. In this case the flexing is obtained by means of spring steel rings inserted between each wooden spoke and the wheel rim. In spite of their apparent flexibility, however, the Sté. Française des Automobiles Corre seemingly dared not dispense with the habitual suspension by semi-elliptic leaf springs.

The frame is built up of brazed tubes; transmission is through a leather-covered cone clutch, three-speed gearbox, and drive shaft to the rear axle. The Corre in Rochetaillée has been beautifully restored—perhaps too beautifully for a 1904 machine, although it is splendid to look at.

Rolland-Pilain
1909

A generous use of curved surfaces characterizes this French roadster. Its 2.2-liter four-cylinder side-valve engine is neatly installed.

Rolland was the most widely known of the Tours-based Pilain family. In fact, his name was featured in the marque. However, there were others, such as his brother François, who was engineering manager for the first four years, and Emile Pilain, who was with the company in its last years.

The car in the Rochetaillée museum is an interesting derivative of the 1908, 1,526-cc-engined racing roadster, with which the firm first tried to make a name for itself in the 1908 Grand Prix des Voiturettes at Dieppe. Dated as 1909, the car at Rochetaillée has been fitted with a larger, 2.2-liter engine, a neat cowling, rakish fenders, lights, horn, and other road equipment, making it an effective early two-seater sports car.

This Rolland-Pilain probably figured in hillclimbs at the time, since its gear ratios are better suited to twisting grades than to high-speed circuits. The engine is a front-mounted, in-line sleeveless Four in cast iron, with side valves. Dimensions are 80x110-mm bore and stroke, giving 2,211 cc. Maximum power is about 22 horsepower.

Water cooling, aided by a fan, is employed and there is magneto ignition and a single-barrel vertical carburetor. The sump is of cast aluminum, a three-speed gearbox is used, and final drive is by propeller shaft.

The frame is unusual, appearing to be straight in side view, but, in fact, the longitudinal members broaden out behind the engine to the width of the two side-by-side seats. Suspension is by the usual semi-elliptics fore and aft, and there are wooden-spoked wheels and wooden rims, mounting 760x90 tires. The handbrake works on rear drums, the footbrake on the driveline.

In several ways this sporting machine was ahead of its time, as in the bold form of the body with its curved cowling, the neat, rounded tail, the steeply angled steering column, and the low build, all inherited from racing. Its wheelbase is 105 inches, weight is about 1320 lbs. (600 kg), and, with road equipment, the car could attain a maximum speed of 62 mph (100 kph).

The racing origins of this Rolland Pilain are obvious in its lines, from the rudimentary fenders to the air-deflecting cowling and staggered seats in the cockpit.

Renault Petit Duc

1910

Renault of Billancourt is today the largest factory in France and one of the oldest; still preserved in the gardens of the management offices is the little workshop where Louis Renault built his very first car in 1898. The 1910 two-cylinder model, like all Renaults produced until the 1920s, has the classic dashboard radiator, with its unmistakable shape, protruding on both sides of the hood. This arrangement made everything very accessible for maintenance.

The twin cylinders have a 70-mm bore and a 110-mm stroke for a total capacity of 846 cc and a declared power er of 8 horsepower, which was not far from its real output. The cylinders are cast in a single block with an L-head and side valves, and water-cooled by thermosiphon circulation. Ignition is by magneto, and the carburetor is of Renault manufacture. Lubrication is by a gravity system with the drip-feed adjusters high on the dashboard.

A leather-covered cone clutch is employed, and the patent Renault four-speed gearbox is separate from the engine, a hangover, perhaps, from the days when chain drive made it more convenient to have the gearbox in unit with the differential. On this little car, however, as with all Renaults from the very first, the final drive is by propeller shaft.

The handbrake shares the same support, with the gear lever in the exposed style usual for the time. The three pedals from left to right are the clutch, accelerator, and brake, the latter working on the transmission.

The channel-section chassis is simple but strong. Suspension all around is by semi-elliptic leaf springs, and the usual wooden-spoked wheels of the era are fitted, carrying 710x90 tires at front and rear. Wheelbase of the 8 horsepower Renault is 98 inches, and the track at front and rear measures 51 inches.

The Petit Duc was a popular open style of body, and the lightness of its construction kept the weight just below 1120 pounds. The maximum speed of this reliable little car on a mere 846 cc was around 28 mph.

With a body reduced to little more than the seats, this car has an excellent power-to-weight ratio—it could reach 28 mph.

58

Léon-Bollée Double Berline

1912

Léon Bollée was the son of the famous Amédée Bollée senior (there was also a son called Amédée), the name that first comes to mind when speaking of French steam vehicles.) Léon began building gasoline-powered motor cars at Le Mans quite early, moving on from tourers to medium horsepower cars.

The 1912 double phaeton on view at Rochetaillée is an extremely elegant vehicle, albeit in a somewhat baroque style, with coachwork that looks as if it were formed of two identical bodies joined together. Its considerable length and general uprightness make it look even larger than it is, the wheelbase being 119 inches and the front and rear tracks 55 inches.

The water-cooled engine of this Léon-Bollée is a twin-block four-cylinder with side-by-side valves, magneto ignition, and a Claudel carburetor. Bore and stroke measure 83x110 mm, and the output is given as 24 horsepower. The cylinder blocks are bolted onto an aluminum crankcase and sump, which is fixed to the longitudinal members of the chassis in order to increase its rigidity. Thermosiphon cooling is employed, and lubrication is by a pump driven by a skew gear.

A leather-faced cone clutch and four-speed gearbox transmit the power through a torque tube to a bevel final drive on the rear axle. Gear selection is by a system of rockers in the gearbox housing. The drop-forged front axle is suspended on semi-elliptic leaf springs, and long semi-elliptic springs are featured at the rear. The wooden artillery wheels have nondetachable rims.

Lighting on this Léon-Bollée is by acetylene gas for the main headlamps, with a centralized generator. There are also auxiliary oil lamps, handsomely ornate and brassy in keeping with the period. The four-door, eight-window, six-seater phaeton bodywork is luxuriously fitted out, at the expense of considerable weight. The car scales 2425 pounds (1,100 kg), restricting top speed to around 40 mph.

This double phaeton with its unconventional bodywork could transport its six occupants at speeds of up to 41 mph with every comfort.

Hotchkiss Torpedo

1922

The badge of the Hotchkiss factory bears two crossed cannons, a clear indication of the activities the firm was engaged in before it started building motor cars. The transition from armament production came about gradually, with the manufacture first of motor parts, and then of complete cars. The name has also been perpetuated in the so-called Hotchkiss drive, the open drive shaft transmission system in which the rear springs provide the axle location and resist drive and braking torque; the alternative system was a torque

Under that not very imposing hood is a sturdy four-cylinder side-valve 4-liter engine that could push this car along at over 60 mph. There is a second windshield to protect the rear seat passengers from the wind. Note the long cantilever leaf spring suspension for the rear axle, attached to the chassis at two points. As an old armaments firm, Hotchkiss incorporated two crossed cannons in its badge.

tube enclosing the propeller shaft and anchored at the forward end.

The 1922 "torpedo"-bodied Hotchkiss to be seen at the Rochetaillée museum is a typical French open ·tourer of the 1920s. It has a four-cylinder side-valve engine, cast as a monobloc in iron. Bore and stroke are 95x140 mm, and capacity is 3,962 cc. Lubrication is by pressure, and the cooling system utilizes a centrifugal pump, radiator, and fan. A Zenith triple-diffuser carburetor ensures the correct mixture, and ignition is by high-tension magneto with variable advance. Reliability rather than high performance is the aim in this car, but an overhead valve version of the engine was also made for competition use.

Use of a leather cone clutch was a dated feature by the 1920s, but Hotchkiss was always conservative in design. The gearbox has four forward speeds and reverse, and transmission is by drive shaft and a Gleason bevel rear axle. The chassis is extremely sturdy and well engineered, as is evident from the deep pressed-steel side members. Front suspension is by semi-elliptic leaf springs, while at the rear are cantilever-type leaf springs, anchored at the center and at the fore-end to the chassis, with the rear end supporting the axle.

There are rear wheel drum brakes, and the wire wheels with central fixing bolt are fitted with 895x135 tires. The track at front and rear measures 55 inches, while the wheelbase is 131 inches, this being the long version of the 4-liter four-cylinder Hotchkiss, also available with a shorter chassis. The weight is a substantial 2860 pounds (about 1,300 kg), and the car could travel at 62 mph (100 kph) with commendable comfort. The open four-seater "torpedo" body has extra screens for the rear passengers.

Grand Prix Rolland-Pilain

1923

It is fortunate that so rare and interesting a racing car as the 2-liter Grand Prix Rolland-Pilain has survived to the present day and can be inspected at Rochetaillée. The Rolland-Pilain factory decided to return to racing in 1922 when the 2-liter GP Formula came into force, and its designer, Grillot, produced a car that deserved more success than the single victory in the 1923 San Sebastian Grand Prix in Spain, where the two Rolland-Pilains came in first and second, driven by Guyot and Delalandre. Every care was taken in the design and construction of these cars, some features of which were well ahead of the times.

The straight-Eight, water-cooled, 1,978-cc engine has a 59.2x90-mm bore and stroke, and develops about 80 horsepower. Gear-driven twin overhead camshafts operate two valves per cylinder set at 45 degrees from vertical. Ignition is by Scintilla magneto, and four Zenith car-

sion is by semi-elliptic leaf springs and rigid axles all around, aided by friction dampers.

Advanced for the time were the hydraulic brakes for the front wheels, made under Duesenberg license. The rear brakes, however, were mechanically operated. The wire wheels were unusual too, being built with the brake drums aligned with the hubs and steering centers, in order to minimize instability under braking.

The bodywork of the racing Rolland-Pilain was smooth and sleek, with a long tail. Unusually for a Grand Prix car, it had left-hand drive.

Below, the four carburetors on the straight-Eight, twin overhead camshaft engine can clearly be seen. This rare survivor from the famous 2-liter formula was capable of 100 mph.

buretors are fitted, each feeding two cylinders. The cylinder block is aluminum with inserted wet liners; the head is cast iron.

Expensive features are the crankshaft built up in 13 sections, to allow ball main bearings and roller-type big ends to be introduced, and extremely light magnesium pistons. Desmodromic valves—a system wherein the valves are shut by a direct mechanism and not, as normally, by a spring—were experimented with by Grillot, but for practical racing use a return to traditional methods was deemed advisable.

Transmission is through a disk clutch, four-speed gearbox, and torque tube drive. The wheelbase is 107 inches, and the chassis side members are set very close together and, unusually, pass under instead of over the rear axle. The car is notably "crab-tracked," with a front track of 47 inches and rear track of 43 inches. Suspen-

FIAT 509 S Barchetta

1926

The FIAT 509 was a very popular Italian car in its time, being lively, compact, and economical, yet with all the accessories and attributes of a larger model. Tens of thousands were built between 1925 and 1929; some were 509S variations, wearing the attractive, open, sporting, two-seater bodywork of the "Barchetta" or "boat" type.

An example of the Barchetta is to be seen at the Rochetaillée museum. The engine is an in-line, four-cylinder unit with detachable head and overhead valves operated by a single chain-driven overhead camshaft. Bore and stroke are 57x97 mm, and total displacement is 990 cc, producing 22 horsepower at 3,400 rpm for the standard 509, or 27 horsepower at 4,000 rpm for the 509S.

Ignition is by a Marelli MR4 magneto; a single vertical carburetor is fitted; and water cooling is by thermosiphon and fan, driven directly off the camshaft through a friction joint. Power is taken through a single dry-plate clutch to a gearbox with only three speeds. This box is in unit with the engine, which is fixed rigidly by four points to the chassis. A torque tube encloses the propeller shaft to the rear axle, the housing for which is fabricated by pressing and welding.

The 509 chassis comprises two straight longitudinal members, cross-braced at three points as well as by the engine-gearbox unit. Suspension is by semi-elliptic leaf springs and friction dampers at front and rear. Rudge-Whitworth quick-release wire wheels mount 27x4.75 tires. Sankey steel wheels or 5-stud wire-type were also optional. Drum brakes are fitted to all four wheels, with the handbrake acting on the rear drums.

The 12-volt electrical system includes a starter, lighting and warning lights for the oil pressure and generator—a system new to Europe, brought over from the United States. There are no instruments at all on the dashboard, which merely has a central control panel including the warning lights. The ignition advance control is in the center of the steering wheel, while the accelerator pedal lies between the larger clutch and brake pedals.

FIAT made a serious effort to reduce servicing to a minimum on the 509 range of models. For example, the generator is driven straight off the front end of the propeller shaft, dispensing with a drive belt; the gas tank is mounted in front of the dashboard, while the oil level can be checked by an indicator on the engine.

66

Wheelbase of the 509S Barchetta is 100 inches, and the car scales some 1450 pounds, compared with around 1740 pounds for the standard 509. Maximum speed with the wooden two-seater body is 57 mph.

This curious and original body for the classic FIAT 509 model is probably the only one of its kind in existence today.

Le Mans Lorraine-Dietrich

1925

In 1908 the ancient engineering concern of de Dietrich, whose cars figured prominently in racing at the beginning of the century, added to their name that of the region where the factory was and embodied the cross of Lorraine into their badge. After World War I, Lorraine-Dietrich introduced a range of finely built 15 CV six-cylinder touring cars of excellent performance. The Le Mans Lorraine-Dietrich, which was designed by Marius Barbarou, was developed at their factory and proved highly successful in the early Le Mans 24-Hour Races.

The famous race was confined in its first years to production sporting cars, and the Lorraines took second and third places in 1924, first and third in 1925, and first, second, and third in 1926. It is claimed that the car at Rochetaillée is the actual one that won at Le Mans in 1925, in which case it has been much altered since, to the detriment of its appearance. Different, heavier fenders and oversize tires of the wrong kind both spoil the "restoration," but beneath the unauthentic though still handsome exterior lies the real heart of a Le Mans Lorraine-Dietrich.

The engine is an in-line, water-cooled Six with overhead valves operated by exposed pushrods and rockers. The bore and stroke are 75x130 mm, and displacement is 3,446 cc. There is copious pressure lubrication with two special oil coolers, twin Zenith horizontal carbure-

The dashboard certainly suggests this car was used for racing. There is a tachometer in front of the driver, while well in view are the mileage counter, a 24-hour clock, and temperature gauge, all instruments added for a particular purpose. The Lorraine's combination of high speed (93 mph) and reliability brought it great success at Le Mans.

tors, and dual distributor and coil ignition. The 15 CV quoted in France is the fiscal horsepower, but the effective brake horsepower must have been well over 70 at about 3,500 rpm.

The transmission is by a multi-plate clutch, a gearbox with, surprisingly, only three speeds, and torque tube final drive. Specially powerful Perrot-type brakes with a Dewandré servo were fitted for Le Mans by Barbarou. The sturdy pressed steel frame has semi-elliptic front springs and long, splayed cantilever leaf springs at the rear, with friction dampers all around. The body is a four-seater, as was compulsory at Le Mans in the 1920s, and was originally of boat-tail type, regretfully missing from the car at Rochetaillée.

Wheelbase is 113 inches, track 57 inches, and weight just over 2350 pounds. The performance and road-holding of the Le Mans cars were highly impressive, and their robustness proved ideal for the long, arduous race.

Bugatti Type 35B

1929

There have been many fine Bugattis, but probably the finest of them all was the Type 35B, distinguished by the exceptional purity of its lines and by its outstanding success in motor racing between 1925 and 1931.

It was launched in 1924 as the Type 35 with a 2-liter engine, when Bugatti ran a works team of five in the Grand Prix of Europe at Lyons. The capacity was raised to 2,262 cc (60-mm bore and 100-mm stroke) in the Type 35T built for the 1926 Targa Florio. The Type 35B was developed from this car, the engine capacity remaining unchanged, but with the addition of a supercharger that raised the power output from about 115 to 135 horsepower at 5,300 rpm.

The engine typifies Bugatti artistry and workmanship in every detail. The cylinder block and head are cast square in light alloy and highly polished. The sump is divided along the axis of the crankshaft, which runs in five ball and roller bearings. For each cylinder there are three vertical valves (two inlets and one exhaust), and all are operated by a single shaft-and-bevel driven overhead camshaft. The oil sump has a series of 13 copper pipes running through it longitudinally to admit cooling air. The supercharger is a Roots-type, mounted on the off-side, while the magneto, driven off the rear of the camshaft, protrudes into the cockpit behind the firewall.

The slim, elegant lines of the car are matched by the exquisitely formed horseshoe radiator. The chassis is a masterpiece of design, the depth swelling out from the delicate front spring supports to meet the varying stresses, then tapering down again at the rear, while it also conforms to the body shape. The wheelbase is 94 inches, the front track 49 inches, and the rear track 47 inches. The unladen weight is around 1700 pounds, and the maximum speed is between 120 and 125 mph. Apart from its beautiful shape the most destinctive feature of the Type 35 is its cast alloy, flat-spoked wheels with integral brake drums.

The Bugatti 35B was capable of over 120 mph, and its liveliness and reliability made it the choice of many racing drivers in the late 1920s. The supercharged, single overhead camshaft engine developed 135 horsepower.

Delage D8

1929

Louis Delage began like many other great designers, working in a car factory, and then setting up on his own. Although the make no longer exists, it survived from 1905 to 1954, and nearly all the models it produced were de luxe, or certainly out of the ordinary.

The D8, a touring example that can be seen at Henri Malartre's museum at Rochetaillée, is a large and outstandingly elegant car with a large, sleeveless, straight-Eight engine, water-cooled, and with overhead valves operated by pushrods and rockers. An interesting refinement is that the valve springs operate separate rocker arms in order to reduce valve bounce.

With a 77x109-mm bore and stroke, the total displacement is 4,060 cc, and the power is 80 horsepower in the version at Rochetaillée, or 90 horsepower at 3,400 rpm for a more sporting edition designated the D8S. The maximum speed was 80 mph (130 kph). The car has coil

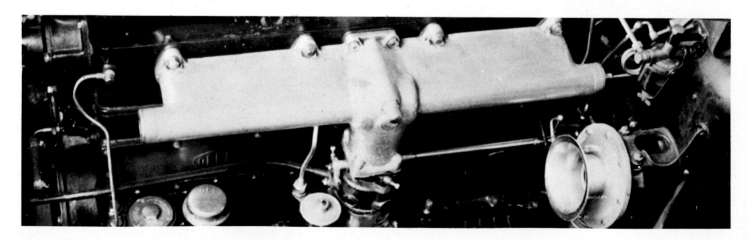

In the days of the "grandes marques" among motor cars, a sign of distinction was the statue on the radiator cap. On this imposing Delage D8 the statue also incorporates the thermometer.

and distributor ignition, and the cooling system is by pump, fan, and radiator. The engine has very thorough pressure lubrication, and gas is fed to the carburetor by a vacuum system.

There is a dry-plate clutch; the four-speed gearbox is in unit with the engine; and a spiral bevel final drive is used. The wire wheels carry 6.50x18 tires. This D8 model is the largest that Delage made. Its wheelbase is 143 inches, and the tracks are 57 inches front and rear. Considering that it is an open car, the Rochetaillée ex-

ample is heavy too, with a weight of 3175 pounds.

The Delage D8 was first presented at the 1929 Paris Motor Show, but, in practice, production did not begin until 1930, when it was made available with various lengths of wheelbase to allow different types of body to be mounted. Such a fine, large chassis was naturally popular with the great French coachbuilders of the day. Subsequently, lower and still more elegant Delages emerged from the Courbevoie factory in Paris, until the market for big, expensive luxury models began to dry up in the late 1930s. By then the D8 embodied several improvements, including synchromesh gearboxes and hydraulic brakes. Today, examples of these handsome Delages are treasured in many museums.

73

Voisin C14

1932

Gabriel Voisin, a Gallic rival to the Wright brothers, was already famous for his airplanes when he decided to engage in manufacturing cars after World War I. He launched numerous models renowned for their technical excellence. These were recognizable by the bird motif on their distinctive vee radiators.

The unusual looking C14 two-door saloon, which is one of Malartre's prized exhibits at Rochetaillée, has a six-cylinder engine with sliding sleeve valves of Knight type made under license, which ensure extremely quiet running. It has a 67x110-mm bore and stroke and 2,327-cc overall capacity, being the smallest engine built in that period by Voisin, when it was even producing a 4.8-liter 12-cylinder model at Issy-les-Moulineaux.

Its cylinders are cast in two blocks of three, bolted to the crankcase, which contains the camshaft driving the sleeves. The C14 had its power expressed as a double figure; that is, the fiscal power and the effective power, hence 16/50. The unit is water-cooled with thermo-siphon circulation; ignition is by coil, distributor, and battery; and fuel feed is via a Zenith carburetor, with a pump drawing the gasoline forward from the rear-mounted tank.

The clutch is of the multi-plate type. The gearbox most ingeniously offers a choice of three or six speeds, by means of an overdrive between the gearbox and the rear axle, which provides a lower set of ratios for hill-climbing or slow traffic work, and is worked by a push-button on the dashboard. Final drive is by spiral bevel, with a ratio of 5 to 1. Voisin-Dewandré servo brakes are fitted all around.

Suspension is by semi-elliptic leaf springs to both axles, and the disk wheels mount 6.50x18 tires. Voisin often made its own bodywork, which was very light and practical, but unfortunately eccentrically ugly, which restricted sales of this excellent car. The wheelbase is 130 inches, and overall weight 2890 pounds (1,310 kg). Thus the maximum speed of 74.5 mph (120 kph) was an excellent performance on a 2.3-liter sleeve-valve engine.

The austere, square lines of this car hardly suggest speed, yet it could exceed 70 mph comfortably with an engine of only 2.3 liters.

75

Hispano-Suiza T12

1934

The proud name of Hispano-Suiza derives from a combination of the Spanish words for "Spanish" and "Swiss," for the make's first factory (still in existence today) was in Barcelona, and its designer, Marc Birkigt, was a Swiss. Generally, however, it is better remembered as a French make, for its cars were also built in Paris.

Most exotic of the French-built Hispano-Suizas was the 12-cylinder, which was produced from 1931 to 1938. For sheer magnificence, performance, and price, it had few peers in its day. The twelve cylinders are arranged in to banks of six at an angle of 60 degrees, with independent accessories for each row; thus there were two water pumps, two magnetos, and so on. A single camshaft, located in the center of the vee in the crankcase, operated the overhead valves by means of pushrods and rockers.

The cylinder heads and blocks are cast integrally in aluminum alloy, with Nitralloy steel liners. Cylinder dimensions are "square," with a 100-mm bore and 100-

mm stroke giving an impressive total displacement of 9,425 cc, making it the largest engine then in production anywhere, although by 1935 an 11.3-liter version was available! A seven-bearing crankshaft, tubular connecting rods, and light alloy pistons are used, and power output is an effortless 220 horsepower at 3,000 rpm, with a compression ratio of only 5 to 1. A multi-plate clutch takes this formidable power through a gearbox with only three speeds. It is significant, however, that the ratio of the lowest gear is 5.4:1, or much the same as the highest ratio on many cars—a fact made possible by the enormous power and flexibility of the V-12 engine.

That great engine, and the overall weight of the car (over 2,200 kg, or 4,851 pounds!) requires an extremely sturdy chassis, which uses semi-elliptic springs on both axles. Four wheelbases were available, between 135 inches and 158 inches. The brakes are immensely powerful servo-mechanical, and the wire wheels carry 700x19 tires. The classic Hispano-Suiza radiator, one of the most elegant ever evolved, has thermostatically-controlled shutters, while on the radiator cap is poised the famous swan with its great wings beating down in flight. The Coupe de Ville body on the car at the Rochetaillée museum is a classic example of its kind, exquisitely proportioned and graceful.

One of the great classics among large, sporting luxury makes is Hispano-Suiza, and its graceful flying swan radiator mascot is one of the loveliest of all. Every line in this Coupe de Ville is superbly elegant.

Grand Prix Lago-Talbot

1949

The racing cars built at the Talbot factory at Suresnes, Paris, by the French-based Italian designer Antonio Lago gained numerous Grand Prix successes in the years 1948-51, thanks to the relatively simple design formula followed in their construction. Instead of exploiting the greater power offered by the 1,500-cc supercharged engine permitted under the first Formula One, Lago went to the other extreme of the rules, choosing a big six-cylinder engine with no supercharger.

This meant a less complex, if less powerful, but more reliable power unit consuming only half as much fuel as the blown cars. Thus in most races the Talbot-Lagos only had to make one refueling stop to their rivals' two, saving time at the pits, which the supercharged cars had to

The engine (below) of the Talbot-Lago has three twin-choke carburetors. It looks as though it has twin overhead camshafts, but these are, in fact, in the cylinder block and operate the valves by short pushrods and rockers in two separate covers.

make up by extra speed. These virtues won Talbot the French, Belgian, and Dutch Grands Prix in addition to numerous lesser events.

The Talbot six-cylinder racing engine is derived from a similar type built before World War II, with the dimensions brought up to a 93x110-mm bore and stroke and a displacement of 4,483 cc. The most interesting feature is the overhead valve gear, with two camshafts located one each side of the block and set high to allow the use of short pushrods. This simple system allowed the head to be stripped down without touching the timing system. Power output was about 275 horsepower at 5,000 rpm, obtained on a gasoline-based mixture, with three Zenith twin-barrel carburetors that received air from a prominent inlet tube on the off-side of the hood.

The gearbox, too, is unusual for a Grand Prix car, being of Wilson epicyclic type with pre-selector. With this heavy but useful kind of box, the driver would pre-select the gear he required by means of a lever on the steering column just beneath the wheel, then when he depressed the clutch pedal the gear was changed without his having to remove his hands from the steering wheel, thus saving time and energy.

The chassis is a simple, rugged structure, with channel steel side members and independent front suspension by a transverse leaf spring and stout wishbones. At the rear there is a rigid axle with semi-elliptic leaf springs. This was old-fashioned by that time, but strong, dependable, and inexpensive. Houdaille hydraulic shock absorbers are fitted all around, and brakes are Bendix mechanical.

The single-seater body is well-proportioned with the driver seated low and the transmission offset thanks to a pair of spur gears. Tires are 5.50x18 front and 6.50x18 rear; the wheelbase is 98.5 inches, front track 54 inches, and rear track 51.5 inches; the unladen weight was over 2,000 pounds, which was heavy for a Grand Prix car.

DAIMLER BENZ MUSEUM

The Daimler-Benz museum at Stuttgart-Untertürkheim forms part of a large complex of buildings comprising the head-quarters of the famous German Mercedes-Benz factory. It also houses all the records and relics of historic importance relating to those two founders of German car manufacture, Gottlieb Daimler and Carl Benz, and to the products of their respective makes, which finally amalgamated to form a single enterprise in 1926.

A three-story building, standing alongside the general management offices, has housed the Daimler-Benz museum since 1961, the year in which it was given its permanent home to commemorate the 75th anniversary of the first horseless carriages produced by the two pioneers—carriages that were the world's first practical motor cars, and that pointed the way for all subsequent automobiles.

Preserved in this museum is the first authentic Daimler car, built in 1886, alongside a careful copy of the Benz vehicle produced at the same time, the original of which belongs to the Deutsches Museum in Munich. Both Daimler's and Benz' first engines, the one vertical, the other horizontal, typify the first interpretations of the Otto four-stroke internal combustion gasoline engine. Development of the Daimler for use in an airship followed, but all that remains of the first aeronautical application of this historic engine is a faded photograph, which, nevertheless, is very important, as are relics of its railway and naval applications.

The Benz Velo (the world's first production car), the Victoria (which made a 700-mile journey to France in 1895), the Ideal, various Daimler vehicles, and many Mercedes from 1902 onward mark a whole series of milestones and memories; one is the Mercedes-Knight with sleeve-valve motor, which the Daimler Company built on Knight patents, another is the famous 8/95 sports car of 1914.

Following the merger of Daimler and Benz, a new series of models went into production; there was the Mannheim and the Stuttgart, after the cities where the two firms had their headquarters, the Nurburg, the SS and SSK, proud bearers of the three-pointed star emblem with the new name—Mercedes-Benz.

The sporting section on the second floor is particularly interesting, for here can be seen the racing cars and record breakers that have become legendary—the great 200-horsepower Blitzen Benz, the 1914 Mercedes, which scored first, second, and third places in the French Grand Prix, the sleek Silver Arrows, which dominated motor racing in the late 1930s, and the postwar sports and racing cars that so ably carried on the winning legend of Mercedes-Benz.

The curator of the museum, Alfred Neubauer, is an exceptional man. He began his career as a racing driver and then became the team manager for Mercedes-Benz, directing the German cars to innumerable victories between 1926 and 1955. Neubauer was the archetype of all team managers; his strict discipline and meticulous supervision of all aspects of racing was a guarantee of success. Despite his stern approach he was like a father to his drivers, understanding their inner tensions.

So Neubauer remains with his cars, ensuring that the countless visitors to the museum see them in all their perfection, though they no longer perform on the racing circuits and their superb engines are silent.

Daimler Motor Carriage

1886

Gottlieb Daimler, a brilliant engineer, pioneered along with Karl Benz in the development of the automobile. Daimler's critical contribution was in the practical application of Nikolaus Otto's four-stroke engine. After working with Otto for ten years, Daimler went on to develop his own high-speed version of the engine, and with Wilhelm Maybach's help succeeded in evolving a power unit that was light, compact, and efficient.

In 1886 Daimler produced the first four-wheeled car around this engine, which you see here. The body was simply a carriage set in motion by Daimler's internal combustion engine rather than by a horse. Wimpff & Son of Stuttgart supplied the carriage, which Daimler had ordered as a present for his wife since he wanted to keep his experiment secret. He had the engine fitted into it at an engineering works in Esslingen.

Daimler's engine was the direct ancestor of the modern power unit. It had a single vertical cylinder measuring 70-mm bore and 120-mm stroke, giving a capacity of 462 cc, and around 650 rpm it gave approximately 1.1 horsepower. It ran on benzine, which was vaporized in a surface carburetor and taken into the engine via an automatic suction-operated inlet valve. Immediately below, and sharing the same tract, was the exhaust valve, activated by a rod which itself was worked by a double cam-groove in one of the two flywheels.

Ignition was by the very first "hot tube," devised by Daimler and Maybach, consisting of a platinum tube screwed into the combustion chamber and maintained at red heat by a Bunsen burner. The engine was water-cooled, with a large radiator mounted at the back of the car. Lubrication was on the "splash" principle.

Emphasizing that this vehicle was a compromise to test out a new principle, the engine was installed in the middle of the car, between the front and rear seats! It transmitted the drive to the rear wheels by a complex system of belts and internally toothed gears fixed to the spokes of the large artillery-type rear wheels. Two forward speeds were achieved by means of a pair of independent belts held taut at will by means of jockey pulleys.

For steering, the whole of the front axle turned on a central pivot in true carriage fashion. Moreover, the classic fully elliptic leaf spring suspension was retained, as was primitive braking on the rim of the rear wheels.

It was nothing more than a horseless carriage, but the secret lay in the engine that replaced the horse—the first practical, light gasoline engine, strong enough to drive the carriage at 9 mph. The total weight of the Daimler is about 1,320 pounds, one-third of it accounted for by the new mechanism mounted on it—a ratio similar to that maintained today.

Benz Mylord Coupe
1897

The early Benz cars are as interesting as the early Daimlers. Among the historic cars in the company museum is the Mylord Coupe, a super-luxury enclosed four-wheeler with folding top. Its engine has twin horizontally opposed cylinders, a type of unit with very good balance. First it was called the Kontra motor; later it acquired the generic name Boxer.

Bore and stroke of the Mylord's engine are 120x120 mm, giving a total displacement of 2,714 cc. The power output is 9 horsepower at 900 rpm, which was raised on later models to 10 horsepower. The engine is water-cooled, carburetion is by Benz's own surface vaporizer, and the spark plugs were also made by Benz, with low-tension ignition by condenser and coil.

The flat-Twin engine is easily accommodated below the carriage body, just ahead of the rear wheels. Transmission is by a series of belts and stepped pulleys providing three forward speeds and reverse to a countershaft which, in turn, transmits the rotational energy to a differential. On either side of the differential are drive sprockets controlling the drive chains to both rear wheels.

The driver sits exposed at the front, his tiller and controls grouped around a vertical steering column. The styles of the body, wheels, and suspension are reminiscent of horse-drawn carriages—Benz designs remained conservative to the turn of the century.

The Mylord was fairly short at 114 inches overall, with a track of fractionally over 49 inches, and the very large artillery-spoked wheels had solid rubber tires instead of the pneumatics then becoming popular. Braking was by pedal to the countershaft, and by hand-operated "spoon" brake to the rear wheel rims. Speed was close to 25 mph. The car was reliable for its day, and in the dawn of the motoring era its design was widely copied until superseded by vehicles of more advanced concept with front-mounted engines.

This Benz has 19th-century lines and a complicated but compact power train.

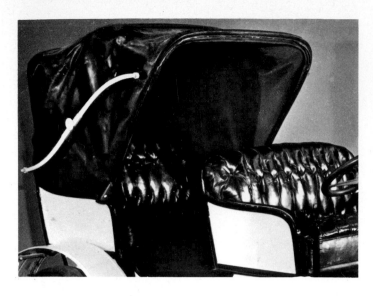

Mercedes Simplex 40/45

1902

The choice of the name Mercedes for its cars brought the Daimler Motoren Gesellschaft good fortune. It was pleasant and easy on the ear, and the first model to bear this girl's name, the 35 horsepower of 1901, proved widely acceptable even to those who had no great liking for Germany or its products.

The Mercedes Simplex models of 1902 were developed versions of the first series, with a choice of several engine sizes, for example, the version in the Daimler-Benz museum is called the 40/45. Its engine has four cylinders cast in pairs, with a bore and stroke of 118x150 mm, giving an overall capacity of 6,786 cc. The maximum power of 44 horsepower was realized at 1,300 rpm with a smoothness and flexibility that was outstanding for 1902.

Here is one of the finest cars of its day, capable of no less than 43 mph and proud possessor of an excellent reputation for reliability and racing performance. After the Simplex, all German Daimler cars and subsequently Daimler-Benz models bore the proud name of Mercedes.

The engine has a T-head with side valves, the inlets on one side, the exhausts on the other, mechanically operated by two camshafts in the crankcase. These camshafts are driven by external spur gears, which also work the water pump and the Bosch low-tension magneto. The water cooling is by honeycomb radiator (invented by Maybach), which appeared the previous year on the 35 horsepower model. Another advanced feature for the time was the use of the exhaust gases to pressurize the fuel feed from the rear tank to the carburetor.

The transmission embodied the famous Mercedes scroll-type clutch, having a single spiral spring, and the gearbox had a contemporary four forward speeds and reverse, with another feature pioneered by Mercedes—the gate-type gearchange. Power passes through a differential mounted on a countershaft to the final drive, which is via side chains.

The chassis has full-length pressed-steel side members (pioneered by Mercedes the previous year) and semi-elliptic leaf springs for front and rear axles. The wooden-spoked artillery-type wheels are of almost equal size, carrying 910x90-mm tires at the front and 920x120-mm at the rear. Braking is by two transmission brakes, novel in being water-cooled, and by drum brakes on the rear chain sprockets. The wheelbase is 96 inches, and the track 57 inches. These Mercedes were fairly complicated but very advanced cars, setting a design pattern destined to be widely copied by other manufacturers.

Grand Prix Mercedes

1914

The 4.5-liter racing Mercedes, which scored a shattering success in the 1914 French Grand Prix by taking the first three places, is a curious mixture of technical excellence and conservatism, which can only be explained by a desire not to risk features that had not, at the time, been properly tested—for example, front wheel brakes and twin overhead camshafts.

Its engine, an in-line, four-cylinder unit with a bore and stroke of 93x165 mm, giving 4,483 cc, is derivative of Mercedes' aircraft engine precepts with its separate cylinders machined from steel forgings, with welded-on ports and water jackets. There are four valves to each cylinder, two inlet and two exhaust, operated by a single overhead camshaft and exposed rocker arms. This camshaft is driven from the crankshaft by a vertical shaft and bevel gears, while a cross shaft drives a three-chamber oil pump unit and twin Bosch high-tension magnetos.

Ignition is extremely thorough, with no less than three plugs for each cylinder (with provision for a fourth!), while German thoroughness is also evident in the counter-balanced crankshaft and the pressure lubrication, which includes tiny pipes carried on the connecting rods feeding oil to the wrist pins. The carburetor is of special Mercedes design with barrel-type choke on a Y-branch manifold.

The power output is 115 horsepower at 2,800 rpm, and this is transmitted through a small-diameter double-cone clutch and a separate four-speed gearbox. Final drive is by propeller shaft with twin ring gears and pinions on each side of the differential. The object of this unusual arrangement was to permit slightly angled half-shafts and an outward inclination of the rear wheels to give better tire grip on crowned roads; the system was actually patented by the Daimler Company as early as 1899.

One of the superb white cars which scored a sensational 1-2-3 victory in the 1914 French Grand Prix, this is a racing thoroughbred in every sense, its slender, almost delicate lines pared down to the minimum in the search for lightness and efficiency. But for the absence of front brakes, which were not generally adopted until after World War I, this could be a 1920 car. Maximum speed for the startlingly light (reputedly well under 1,500 pound) car was around 112 mph.

Suspension of the Grand Prix Mercedes is by semi-elliptic leaf springs aided by the makers' own special adjustable shock absorbers; steering is by worm and nut, and although front wheel braking was not used, there are powerful lever-operated rear drum brakes and an external-contracting footbrake on the drive shaft. Quick-release wire wheels carry 820x120-mm tires in front and 895x135-mm at the rear. This car's superb proportions are set off by its striking white finish—Germany's racing color. It carries the racing number of the 1914 GP-winning car.

Mercedes 1.5-liter Sports Car

1921

One of the world's most important sports cars from the technical point of view, the 1.5-liter four-cylinder twin-camshaft Mercedes introduced supercharging to the public in the early 1920s. Its engine reflected racing and aeronautical experience, having four steel cylinders with welded water jackets, and twin overhead camshafts driven by a vertical shaft at the rear of the engine, as on the 1914 Grand Prix car.

Bore and stroke are 65x113 mm, which would seem to date the example in the Untertürkheim museum at 1923, since the earlier supercharged model measured 68x108 mm (besides only having a single overhead camshaft). Total displacement of the model in the museum is 1,499 cc, and its nominal power output is given as 25 horsepower at 2,500 rpm, or around 40 horsepower with the supercharger engaged.

This component forces air through the carburetor, thus the mixture is compressed into a more volatile mixture prior to entering the cylinders. It was engaged at will by the driver when he wanted maximum speed by full depression of the accelerator pedal, which actuated the supercharger through a clutch. The same system was applied to the subsequent Mercedes-Benz SS models, and on the smaller 1.5-liter car it could produce sudden extra performance when revving hard.

Transmission on the 1.5-liter Mercedes is through a double-cone-type clutch derived from the 1914 racing car, a separate four-speed gearbox, and torque tube final drive. The suspension takes the customary form, with rigid axles and semi-elliptic leaf springs all around, assisted by friction shock absorbers. The car has two wheel brakes only (although four-wheel braking was used on the earlier racing 1.5-liter car of 1922). Rudge-Whitworth-type quick-release wire wheels carry 765x 105-mm tires, which are out of scale for the period. One suspects that the fenders, too, are more modern on this restored car. The wheelbase is 103.5 inches, track 51.5 inches, the weight around 1,760 pounds, and the maximum speed 68 mph with supercharger engaged.

This supercharged Mercedes was very advanced for its day.

Targa Florio Mercedes

1924

A Mercedes was the first racing car built in Europe to be fitted with a supercharger. This was the 1923 four-cylinder 2-liter car that raced with minor success at Indianapolis that year. The design was improved by D. Ferdinand Porsche, and in 1924 was successful in winning Europe's most grueling road race, the Targa Florio in the Sicilian mountains.

The actual winning car is displayed at the Daimler-Benz museum today. In several ways it is an enlargement of the earlier 1.5-liter car described on pages 90–91. Its four-cylinder twin overhead camshaft engine has a 70-mm bore and a 129-mm stroke, giving a total capacity of 1,985 cc; maximum power is 120 horsepower at 4,500 rpm.

The two overhead camshafts operate four valves to each cylinder, two inlet and two exhaust. A vertical shaft and beveled gears drive the camshafts, the water pump and the Bosch high-tension magneto. One 18-mm spark plug per cylinder is used. The supercharger is mounted vertically at the front of the engine, driven off the nose of the crankshaft. As on the 1.5-liter engine, it blows through the carburetor. In typical Mercedes fashion the cylinder block is of steel with integral head and welded steel water jackets, while the crankcase is of aluminum.

The clutch is of Mercedes double-cone type, transmitting to a four-speed gearbox separate from the engine, with propeller shaft final drive to the rear axle. Suspension all around is non-independent by semi-elliptic leaf springs, bound with cord and assisted by Mercedes drum-type shock absorbers.

The side members of the chassis are of pressed steel, curved at front and rear to sweep over the axles. Braking is to all four wheels, the drums having attractive dished aluminum backplates, assisted by a transmission brake. On the original car the outside exhaust system passed through an outer funneled section to obtain a scavenging effect, but this is now missing. Wheelbase of the Targa Florio Mercedes is 105.5 inches, weight about 2,600 pounds laden, and maximum speed close to 100 mph.

Christian Werner drove this Mercedes to victory in the 1924 Targa Florio.

Mercedes-Benz Type 770

1930

The largest Mercedes from the aspect of sheer engine size was not, as many people believe, and as its name suggests, the 7.7-liter Grosser Mercedes-Benz of the 1930s, since even before World War I the famous German make had built cars with engines of greater displacement. Yet the Type 770 was the first Mercedes to be tagged with the name—and carried it with distinction.

As can be judged from the example to be seen in the Daimler-Benz museum at Untertürkheim, it is certainly an imposing car. It has a huge eight-cylinder, in-line engine with 95-mm bore and 135-mm stroke, giving a total displacement of 7,655 cc. Fuel consumption was a matter of secondary importance with a car such as this, used by high officials, diplomats and politicians, and it was probably little more than 16 miles per gallon.

For normal road work, the engine gave approximately 150 horsepower at a silky 2,800 rpm but this Jekyll-

This massive open car, intended for ceremonial occasions and parades, has sockets for standards and is partially armor-plated. Despite their weight these monsters could reach 100 mph, thanks to the 7.7-liter engine and a supercharger that could be engaged at will.

and-Hyde motor car was fitted with the "engaged at will" Mercedes supercharger, so that when the occasion merited it, the chauffeur pressed the accelerator pedal right down, boosting the power to a more audible 200 horsepower, still at 2,800 rpm, and a maximum speed of 100 mph.

Its engine is an impressive piece of engineering, with overhead valves operated by a gear-driven overhead camshaft, twin magneto ignition and, of course, the special Mercedes *kompressor* supercharging system, blowing through the carburetor as usual. There is a massive nine-bearing crankshaft, aluminum pistons, and copious pressure lubrication via a gear-driven pump. The engine is water-cooled by pump with thermostatic control, the typical Mercedes-Benz vee radiator having unusual diagonal slats.

Transmission is through a multi-plate clutch and

synchromesh four-speed gearbox, third gear being in direct drive and fourth, in effect, an overdrive. Final drive to the rear wheels is by propeller shaft. The chassis is a massive structure with side members of U-section pressed steel, and suspension on this first Grosser is non-independent by semi-elliptic springs all around.

Servo-assisted brakes are fitted, and these, indeed, are necessary when one considers that the car, even empty, weighs close to three tons, and one armor-plated saloon built for Hitler weighed about 4 tons! The wheelbase is 147.5 inches, and the wheels have 7x20-inch tires. Later Grosser models had independent suspension all around, with swing axles at the rear, and tube-steel chassis.

Mercedes-Benz W25

1934

The Mercedes-Benz W25 racing car marked the return to the Grand Prix circuits of the German firm in what can be considered a golden age of motor racing, beginning in 1934 with the 1,654-pound weight formula. Design of this car was in the hands of two former Benz technicians, Dr. Nibel and Engineer Wagner, who completed their task in about a year. The car to be seen at Untertürkheim is one of the early versions as it appeared in June 1934, with straight-Eight supercharged engine measuring 78x88-mm bore and stroke (3,360 cc), and giving 302 horsepower at 5,800 rpm, or 354 horsepower running on alcohol.

In construction the engine follows techniques developed by Mercedes over many years, using forged-steel cylinders in two blocks of four, with welded-in valve ports and water jackets. Gear-driven twin overhead camshafts operate four valves per cylinder, and the single supercharger is mounted vertically at the front, forcing air through two twin-choke carburetors. Unlike earlier Mercedes, however, the supercharger is permanently engaged.

Much of the engine is made in light alloy; the counter-balanced crankshaft runs in five roller bearings, and the specification includes a single Bosch magneto providing spark to one plug per cylinder. Lubrication is by dry sump.

The chassis of the W25 represents a major advance for its time, having a box-section frame liberally pierced for lightness, and all-independent suspension. At the front this is by coil springs installed horizontally in the tubular front cross member, actuated by bellcranks connected with the wheels. At the rear quarter-elliptic transverse leaf springs control swinging half-axles; friction-type shock absorbers are used, and the brakes are Lockheed hydraulic in 2.75-inch wide aluminum drums, with two separate front and rear circuits.

Yet another unusual design feature of this very advanced racing concept is a gearbox (with four speeds and reverse) built in unit with the rear axle and final drive; the object is to obtain a better weight distribution with the engine mass at the front of the car. All these innovations contributed to a performance that outdated rivals such as Alfa Romeo, Maserati, and Bugatti, the maximum speed of over 160 mph leaving them well behind.

Undoubtedly the superbly streamlined single-seater bodywork of the Mercedes helped its performance; this body was made of light alloy, and even shrouded the suspension, while a driver's head fairing was also fitted. Wheelbase of the W25 is 107 inches, the front track measures 58 inches, while the rear is narrower at 55.5 inches. Unladen weight is 1,875 pounds, the front wheels have 5.25x17-inch tires and the rear 5.25x19-inch.

Later versions of the car had engines enlarged to 3.9 liters, giving an over-170 mph maximum. These superb cars won 11 Grand Prix races in two seasons.

The W25 that wrought such technical changes in Grand Prix racing by its ultra-modern specification and tremendous performance.

These front and rear views of the Grand Prix Mercedes show how its beautiful streamlining encloses protruding parts of the suspension.

This 1934 example is without the driver's head fairing, always used in races. The car weighs 1,875 pounds and could exceed 170 mph.

Mercedes-Benz Record Car

1938

This is one of the cars built by Daimler-Benz with the object of setting new speed records, in this case Class B International (5 to 8 liters), through the flying kilometer and mile. Beneath its fully streamlined exterior, the car is based on the W125 Grand Prix machine raced so

Beneath the beautiful, all-enveloping streamlined shell of this car there is the chassis of a 1937 W125 road-racing Mercedes-Benz with 5.6 liter straight-Eight supercharged engine boosted to give 646 horsepower. Driven by Caracciola on the Frankfurt autobahn, it reached the speed of 268.9 mph, the highest ever achieved on a public road.

successfully during the 1937 season, and it was referred to by the works as the W125R.

The in-line, eight-cylinder supercharged engine has a 94-mm bore and 102-mm stroke, giving an overall cylinder capacity of 5,663 cc. The output, which in the circuit racing version was 592 horsepower at 5,800 rpm, was boosted to 646 horsepower, still at the same number of revolutions, for speed record attempts over comparatively short, straight courses. The increased power was principally due to use of Mercedes' new double-choke, double-jet carburetor called the *schiebervergaser,* which raised the horsepower impressively, but also the fuel consumption—although this was no worry on short-distance record-breaking forays.

Engine construction is the traditional type used by Mercedes for their racing engines, with the cylinders and heads welded in two blocks of four, with welded sheet metal water jackets. The crankshaft runs in nine roller bearings, and four valves per cylinder are operated by twin overhead camshafts. A supercharger is used.

Drive is by open propeller shaft to a four-speed gearbox mounted on the rear axle. Chassis and suspension follow the pattern of the Grand Prix car; that is, a frame of oval tubes, independent front suspension by wishbone links and coil springs, and a de Dion-type tied rear axle with longitudinal torsion bars, and hydraulic double-acting shock absorbers are fitted all around.

The main difference between the record car and the Grand Prix version is obviously in the bodywork. The full-width aerodynamic body of the *Rekordwagen* was designed after exhaustive wind tunnel tests; it encloses the whole vehicle, wheels included, with only a tiny faired screen for the driver. Even the exhaust pipe outlets are carefully shrouded to give minimum drag.

Rudolf Caracciola, the legendary champion of the 1930s, drove this Mercedes-Benz to a shattering new record on the Frankfurt Autobahn at a speed of 268.9 mph—the highest ever recorded in Europe, and the highest speed ever attained on a public highway.

THE DEUTSCHES MUSEUM

There are few museums that inspire a visitor with such pleasurable anticipation as the Deutsches Museum. Situated in the heart of Munich, on a little island on the river Isar, it looks, with its towers and high gray walls, like a medieval castle—although, in fact, it was built in 1903 by the engineer Oscar von Miller.

The museum was founded with the object of creating a complete educational institution covering the diverse fields of technology and the finer sciences. It aimed to make information accessible to the general public on the fundamental laws, the physical phenomena, and the various methods used in the evolution of mechanical science.

Its coverage is wide. It contains examples of important achievements, not only from Germany but also from the whole world

The visitor will find sections dealing with such diverse subjects as underground resources, mines and treatment of minerals, metallurgy, power machines, electricity, hydraulics, land transport, navigation, aeronautics, road, bridge, and tunnel building, physi█ █hemistry, rigid dynamics and meteorology, musical instruments, textile engineering, weights and measures, agricultural technology, astronomy, printing and photography.

In this context the section given over to motor cars may seem rather modest, but it is because one is able to compare cars with other means of transport and mechanisms that it has such interest. There are exhibits of great value and some unique specimens, including an original 1886 Benz, a rear-engined █Rumpler, a 1912 Alpine-type Audi, █nd the spectacular rear-engined

racing Auto Union in chassis form, the sole surviving example.

A new transport hall was opened recently and when studying the first rudimentary means of locomotion and comparing them with later achievements right up to today's automobiles, one cannot help being impressed by the striking progress made in motor vehicle design in comparatively few years.

This is a very complex museum that cannot properly be appreciated in a single day. Many will find it hard to resist examining things like the first naval submarine or the make-up of the sinister V2, forerunner of all missiles. Among the many facilities of the museum there is an extremely efficient bibliographic and diagramatic section, a library, and documentation and study centers.

De Dion 10-hp

1909

The 10-horsepower de Dion model CL with double phaeton body, preserved in the Munich museum and dated 1909, typifies the elegance of design and the precision of detailed construction for which the old-established French firm of de Dion Bouton was so famous. This neat little car has a four-cylinder, in-line, water-cooled monobloc engine, the bore and stroke being 66x100 mm, giving an overall cylinder capacity of 1,368 cc, and a reliable output of 10 to 12 horsepower at 1,500 rpm.

Mechanically operated side valves are employed; cooling is by pump and thermosiphon; and there are dual ignition systems, by Bosch high-tension magneto and coil-and-battery—a useful insurance against failure of one or the other. The engine has pressure lubrication, and there are auxiliary feeds to the gearbox and differential, with an oil tank under the seat and a hand-pump on the dashboard.

Transmission is through a multiple-disk clutch and a separate three-speed gearbox of the *train baladeur* type with straight-through change; third gear is direct. Final drive is by drive shaft to the famous de Dion-type rear axle, in which the differential is fixed rigidly to a chassis cross-tube, with articulated drive shafts to the wheels, tied laterally by a tubular beam, which takes the

Unusual design details of this de Dion to be seen in these photographs are the front end spring shackles (note also the screw-in grease-fittings) and the forked axle ends to support the stub axles. These cars were among the most elegantly engineered of their time.

weight instead of the half shafts. The actual rear springing is by three-quarter semi-elliptics.

Front suspension is by semi-elliptic leaf springs, and these, unusually, are shackled at the front—a well-known de Dion feature of the time. There are internal expanding brakes on the transmission behind the gearbox and on the rear wheels, the shoes of both being interchangeable.

Wooden-spoked artillery type wheels are used, carrying 820x120-mm tires. The de Dion 10 horsepower chassis has pressed steel side members, amply cross-braced by tubes and a sturdy bulkhead. The wheelbase measures 98.5 inches, and the track 44 inches, making the dimensions modest. Yet thanks to the excellent springing, this model gave a notable degree of comfort to its passengers.

The clever ideas and workmanship on this car make it understandable why de Dion Boutons were so popular in their day, yet they were no more expensive than many inferior contemporaries.

Audi Alpensieger

1914

The design is one of classic conception, with an in-line, four-cylinder engine cast in two blocks of two cylinders. The valves are located inlet over exhaust, with pushrod operation from a camshaft gear-driven off a three-bearing crankshaft. The rocker arms for the over-head inlet valves are partly exposed, but the pushrods are enclosed in the block. A single Zenith carburetor is fed fuel from the rear tank by means of exhaust-gas pressure.

Bore and stroke are 90x140 mm, giving a total cylinder capacity of 3,564 cc, and the engine produces 35 horsepower at 1,700 rpm. Water cooling is on the thermosiphon principle, with the fan driven off the crankshaft by a flat belt. The engine has full pressure lubrication with a gear-driven oil pump. A Bosch high-tension magneto fires two spark plugs to each cylinder.

A leather cone clutch transmits the drive to a separate four-speed gearbox, and then through a torque tube to the rear axle.

The chassis has pressed-steel side members, carrying long semi-elliptic leaf spring suspension at front and rear. Brakes operate on the transmission and on the rear wheels; steering is by worm and nut. Rudge-Whitworth-type wire wheels with quick-release hubs are fitted, carrying 820x120-mm tires; the wheelbase is 114 inches. The 2,200-pound car had a top speed of over 55 mph.

The German firm of Audi was founded by August Horch in 1909. Much later in its career, in 1932, it was incorporated into the Auto Union group, and today it is owned, together with NSU, by Volkswagen. One of the most successful models of the early Horch period was the sports Alpensieger, a fine example of which is preserved in the Deutsches Museum at Munich.

Designated the type C14/35, it put up an excellent performance in the pre-World War I Austrian Alpine Trials, winning the team prize both in 1913 and 1914 as well as scoring class wins, hence its name, which means "Alpine winner." It was produced in practically unchanged form from 1912 until 1921.

Twin-block engines were out of fashion by 1914, but the 3.5-liter Audi has one, and also overhead inlet valves and side exhaust valves, with partly exposed rocker arms. This typically Teutonic sports car won the team prize in the Austrian Alpine Trial in 1913 and 1914.

Rumpler Tropfenwagen
1921

Edmund Rumpler began working for the car builder Nesseldorf in Vienna, and then moved to Adler in 1903. Soon he became deeply involved in aircraft design and manufacture, and only after World War I did he return to building cars, locally trying to apply the aeronautical techniques he had learned to land vehicles. His cars were only made in small numbers, however, mostly on an experimental basis. The Rumpler preserved at Munich is one of probably only two examples known to survive, and the only one in original condition, as built between 1921 and 1923.

Nicknamed the Tropfenwagen or "Teardrop car," it is revolutionary throughout, particularly for its time. It has an unconventional, rear-mounted engine placed under the passengers' seats, and independent rear suspension by swinging half-axles, a patented design by Rumpler. The engine has six cylinders arranged in three banks of two, like an inverted broad arrow. The bore and stroke are 74x100 mm, and the overall cylinder capacity 2,580 cc. Siemens and Halske, who built this remarkable engine for Rumpler, claimed an output of 36 horsepower at 2,000 rpm.

It is water-cooled, has overhead valves, aluminum pistons, pressure lubrication with a piston-type pump, magneto ignition, and a 12-volt electrical system. The 3-speed gearbox and final drive are in a single unit with the engine; thus the weight is concentrated around the rear axles. The suspension is unusual too, consisting of a very long cantilever leaf springs, two extending forward to a beam front axle, and two rearward to the independent swing axles.

The chassis resembles a boat in form, being fabricated in metal sheet as a single structure to which the streamlined bodywork is attached. The two spare wheels are slung horizontally in the base of the "boat," and all seats are set between the axles, with the steering column well forward over the front wheels and installed centrally, giving room for a passenger on each side of the driver. Other unusual features include central headlamps, the curved window glass, and the finlike horizontal, fenders. Wheelbase of the Rumpler is 132 inches, and the disk wheels carry 820x120-mm tires.

Renowned for its radically novel aerodynamic shape, the Rumpler might well be taken for an amphibious vehicle. The flat, flared fenders are intended to protect the sides of the car from splashing without creating any aerodynamic resistance. On the right, the unusual engine, with three banks of two cylinders arranged like an inverted broad arrow, is located at the rear underneath the seats.

Auto Union Type C

1936

In 1933 the newly formed German car manufacturing group of Auto Union, which combined the four firms of Horch, Audi, Wanderer, and DKW, decided to take part in Grand Prix racing to the International Formula in operation between 1934 and 1937. Dr. Ferdinand Porsche prepared a remarkable 16-cylinder rear-engined design, which Auto Union took over. The cars were built at Zwickau, in Saxony. The only surviving example known, a 1936 car in chassis form, can be seen today at the Deutsches Museum.

The 1934 GP Formula laid down a maximum weight of 1,653 pounds (without tires, fuel, or oil), but there was no limit on cylinder capacity or other dimensions; thus Porsche prescribed a large, powerful engine. To keep within the weight limit, the German technicians had recourse to materials that were little used at that time, like exotic, but light, magnesium alloys, for the engine and gearbox.

The chassis was revolutionary for the time, being of tubular structure, with Porsche-type independent front suspension by trailing links and torsion bars, and independent rear suspension by swing axles. At first Auto Union used a transverse leaf spring for rear suspension, but this was replaced in 1935 by torsion bars, enclosed within the tubular chassis side members.

The massive engine is a 45-degree V-16, with a single overhead camshaft between the two banks of cylinders that operate the inlet valves directly and the exhaust valves through short cross pushrods and rocker arms. A vertical supercharger is placed at the rear, and the 1936 C-type engine measures 75x85-mm bore and stroke, giving it a formidable total capacity of 6,008 cc and a power output of 520 horsepower at 5,000 rpm. Ignition is by twin Bosch magnetos with one plug per cylinder, carburetion is by two Solex instruments, and lubrication is the dry sump type.

The engine is water-cooled, with the coolant circulating between the engine and the front-mounted radiators by long pipes. Transmission is through a multi-plate clutch to a four-speed gearbox (originally five, on the 1934 cars), which is mounted behind the rear half shafts. The drive goes forward again to a limited-slip differential.

Wheelbase of the Type C is 114.5 inches, and the track 56 inches front and rear. The wire wheels carry huge racing tires of 7x19 on the rear and 5.25x17 on the front. Despite the unusual driving position these cars won numerous races.

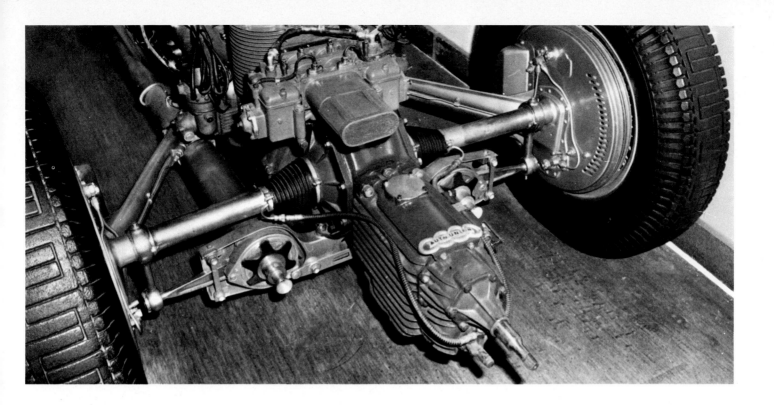

Only the frame and mechanical elements of the Auto Union remain today, and perhaps this is an advantage, for in this way its functional simplicity stands out more clearly. On the left, the finned vertical supercharger can be seen behind the 45 degree 16-cylinder engine.

Horch 853

1938

August Horch, one of the pioneers of the German motor car industry, set up his own factory in Cologne in 1899. In 1904 the firm moved to Zwickau, and in 1932 it was amalgamated with the firms of Audi, Wanderer, and DKW to form Auto Union. Even after this amalgamation the various names were kept to indicate totally different models, and Horch was always the "luxury" member of the group.

The 5-liter straight-eight Horch was built in several variants, of which the Type 853 cabriolet to be seen at the Deutsches Museum is an example. It was built from 1936 to 1939, when war ended the production run. As can be seen, it is an imposing, well-proportioned car in Teutonic style, with a long hood concealing the big in-line, eight-cylinder engine. This has a single overhead camshaft operating overhead valves by rocker arms, and a crankshaft running in ten bearings.

Cylinder dimensions are 87x104-mm bore and stroke, giving a total capacity of 4,944 cc and a power output of 105 horsepower at 3,200 rpm. It is water-cooled and has pressure lubrication, operated by a gear-driven pump; carburetion is by dual Solex instruments, with ignition by coil and distributor.

The Horch transmission is conventional, with a single-disk clutch and the gearbox in unit with the engine. There are four direct speeds and an overdrive providing a fifth ratio. The chassis is a sturdy affair, low-built and with stout cross-bracing. The suspension is independent all around, at the front by a transverse leaf spring and radius arms, and at the rear by a special Horch double-pivot variation on the de Dion system, which employs semi-elliptic leaf springs. Hydraulic shock absorbers are fitted all around.

The Horch 853's big wire wheels have the large diameter hubcaps that were fashionable at the time, and carry 7.50x17-inch tires. Wheelbase of the cabriolet is 139.5 inches and the track 59.5 inches; yet this large luxury car was not expensive at under $2,500.

This de luxe sports model was clearly a rival for the Mercedes-Benz of its day. The long hood and curved landau irons typify the period.

112

Tatra T87

1938

The name Tatra first appeared on automobiles soon after World War I, but the company that manufactured it, the Nesselsdorfer Wagenbaufabrik, was one of the oldest car makers in the Austro-Hungarian Empire, being founded in 1897. The rear-engined T-87, an example of which can be seen at the Munich museum, was the last model to be built by Tatra before the German occupation of Czechoslovakia in 1939; but it was so advanced that it remained the prototype for post-war Tatra cars.

The designer was Hans Ledwinka, an Austrian engineer who spent many years with Nesselsdorf before joining Tatra. His T-87 has two unusual characteristics—its very aerodynamic shape and the rear location of the engine. This engine is an air-cooled V-8, with cylinders measuring 75x84-mm bore and stroke, giving an overall capacity of 2,969 cc and a power output of 72 horsepower at 3,600 rpm.

Cooling is by turbo-fan inside metal shrouding, the cylinder blocks are in cast iron, and the heads and crankcase are in light alloys. Overhead valves are oper-

ated by a single overhead camshaft to each bank of cylinders. The engine is in one unit with the clutch, four-speed gearbox, and differential-cum-final drive. The entire assembly is, therefore, quickly removed for servicing requirements.

The Tatra T-87 was also advanced for its time in having independent suspension to all four wheels. At the front a transverse leaf spring is used in conjunction with upper and lower wishbones, while at the rear the T-87 has swing axles, suspended and located by forward-mounted cantilever springs.

Hydraulic shock absorbers are fitted all around, and the brakes are also hydraulically operated to all four wheels. The pressed-steel wheels carry 6.50x16-inch tires, and the wheelbase is 124 inches. The full-width streamlined bodywork is outstanding for a period when separate fenders and running boards were still fashionable. The rear wheels are enclosed, and there are ducts on each side of the rear trunk to admit cooling air to the engine. The headlights lie flush in the nose, and the Tatra's low aerodynamic drag contributed vitally to its 100-mph maximum speed.

This unusual prewar model from Czechoslovakia foreshadowed things to come so far as its aerodynamics and flush lighting were concerned.

NATIONAL MOTOR MUSEUM

Transferred from the Montagu Motor Museum to magnificent new buildings on a nearby site in 1972, the National Motor Museum is the modern successor to the collection founded by the enthusiastic Lord Montagu of Beaulieu at Palace House, his country seat in a beautiful and historic part of Hampshire, on the edge of the New Forest.

The origin of the collection is interesting. Lord Montagu's father, Lord John, the second Montagu of Beaulieu, was a pioneer of British motoring and one of the politicians who battled for recognition of the early motorist's rights. Edward, the son, inherited his father's keen interest in motoring and began collecting historic cars. His first was the 1903 de Dion originally owned by his father. Finally, he achieved his ambition by founding the Montagu Motor Museum in 1952.

At first the cars were put on show in the hall of Palace House itself, but in 1956 two new display buildings were erected to ease acute pressure on space. The collection expanded as many historic cars came into

Montagu's keeping, and so in 1959 a furher extension was built. As the Montagu Motor Museum thrived, it became increasingly evident that a completely new exhibition hall was required, and the indefatigable Lord Montagu set out to create a National Motor Museum with considerable financial assistance from many members of the British motor industry and associated bodies.

Thus the Beaulieu Museum Trust, a non-profit-making organization, was set up, and construction of the new $1.8 million museum building got under way in 1971. A fresh site further away from the historic Beaulieu house and abbey was prepared, while at the same time a new road was cut through the woods from the Lyndhurst-Beaulieu road, bypassing Beaulieu village and crossing the Beaulieu River by a new three-lane bridge to link with extensive new parking lots hidden discreetly away among the trees just north of the complex.

The new museum, which was opened in July 1972 by HRH the Duke of Kent, is indeed an imposing structure. Designed by eminent architects, the main building covers nearly an acre of ground, providing almost 70,000 square feet of exhibition floor space, and firmly establishing the National Motor Museum among the world's finest exhibition centers.

Over 300 historic vehicles—cars, commercial vehicles, motorcycles, bicycles and so on—are housed in well-lit and airy splendor. Among those represented is the 1895 Knight, one of Britain's first motor vehicles ever; the ever-revered Rolls-Royce Silver Ghost; the 1914 Vauxhall Prince Henry; famous record-breaking cars such as Campbell's first Bluebird of the early 1920s, and Segrave's 1927 1,000-horsepower Sunbeam and 1929 Golden Arrow racing cars such as twincam Austin, E.R.A., Mercedes, and Vanwall; and a wide variety of other cars.

Besides the actual museum, there are restoration workshops, a "processional way" and outdoor arena for rallies, new car displays and so on, an information center with literature and photo library, restaurant and conference building.

Wolseley 6-hp
1904

The Wolseley Company was originally engaged in the manufacture of sheep shearing machinery. It moved tentatively into the motoring field on the initiative of its general manager, Herbert Austin. In 1895 he built his first three-wheeled vehicles, resembling the Léon-Bollée tricar, but Wolseley production in the true sense of the word began in 1900 with a single-cylinder car, soon followed by twin- and four-cylinder models.

The 1904 6-horsepower model to be seen at Beaulieu is technically one of the most interesting of the early Wolseleys. Its single-cylinder engine is mounted horizontally at the front, with its head at the fore-end and the crankshaft across the frame. It has a 114-mm bore and a 127-mm stroke, giving a total engine capacity of 1,302 cc. Power is given variously as 6 or 6.5 horsepower at 800 rpm. The maximum speed attained was a modest 20 mph. From a minimum of 300 rpm, the engine could reach a maximum of 1,000 rpm and was regulated by a hand throttle on the steering column. Unlike many cars of the period, it had no centrifugal speed governor.

The engine is water-cooled with a pump and an unusual radiator composed of banks of horizontal gilled tubes running around the hood. Lubrication is by gravity from an oil tank, with regulator taps, on the dashboard. The ignition, comprised of a proper coil and distributor, was modern for those days. The inlet valve is automatically opened, and the exhaust valve is controlled by a camshaft. As on other Wolseley engines of the time, leaf-type rather than coil valve return springs are used.

The car has a three-speed gearbox mounted separately from the engine, with Renold silent chain transmission between the two, while the clutch is embodied in the gearbox. Another chain transmits the drive to the rear axle. The wooden wheels have 30x3.5-inch tires, and suspension at the front is by semi-elliptic springs. Similar springs are used at the rear together with a transverse leaf. Brakes are of the external contracting type.

The grounds of Beaulieu are a fine setting for the splendor of this Wolseley. Note how the tubular radiator encompasses three sides of the hood with banked rows of finned pipes. Top speed for this car, with 1,301-cc horizontal single-cylinder engine, was around 20 mph.

Grand Prix Austin

1908

It may seem surprising that a make such as Austin should once have taken part in Grand Prix racing, but the famous British company built four cars specially for the 1908 Grand Prix de l'Automobile Club de France. Two of them were chain-driven; two had shaft drive. One of the latter fortunately survived the years and can now be seen on display at Beaulieu. It was the car driven into eighteenth place in the race by J. T. C. Moore-Brabazon (later Lord Brabazon).

The cars were derived from the standard Austin 60 horsepower six-cylinder touring model, which had a "square" engine with 127-mm bore and stroke, and the six cylinders cast singly. Capacity was 9,677 cc, and on the racing versions the power was raised to 100 horsepower at an engine speed of 1,500 rpm. Although the engine size sounds vast, the Austins were in fact the smallest but one on engine capacity in a race that included 12- and 13-liter monsters.

For its period the 100-horsepower Austin, with its long hood and two seats close to the rear axle, is unusually low and elegant. The engine has T-heads and side valves, and dual ignition by means of a high-tension magneto and spark coil. It is water-cooled, with mechanical lubrication. A disk clutch is used, and the four-speed gearbox has its third speed direct, fourth being an overdrive.

The chassis side members are of channel section and the engine is bolted to the extended lower web, thus dispensing with a sub-frame. Suspension is by semi-elliptic leaf springs front and rear, aided by friction shock absorbers. Braking is by a pedal to the transmission and a lever to drum brakes on the rear wheels. The wheels themselves are of the wooden artillery type, carrying Dunlop 880x120 beaded edge tires. The 108-inch wheelbase is long for a racing car, and the track at front and rear is 53 inches.

The fact that the Grand Prix Austins were basically touring cars pitted against specially built racing machines makes the eighteenth and nineteenth places they gained more meritorious than they seem at first. They were well-constructed cars, but undoubtedly their excessive weight and modest horsepower told against them. Moore-Brabazon's car scaled approximately 3,025 pounds to the winner's 2,450 pounds, and although over 90 mph maximum was claimed, its fastest speed through a flying kilometer during the race was 82 mph.

Like other famous makes, Austin tried Grand Prix racing in the great events early in the century, although their 1908 9.7-liter car shown here was based on the standard 60-hp touring Austin with six-cylinder, T-head, side valve engine. Each of the two carburetors has a globular "hot spot" device, utilizing the hot water of the engine to help vaporize the fuel. A maximum speed of over 90 mph was claimed.

Rolls-Royce
Silver Ghost
1909

Originally listed in the catalog as the 40/50, the haunting name Silver Ghost was an apt tribute to the extraordinary noiselessness of this superb car, which has a six-cylinder side-valve engine of legendary smoothness, and a body built chiefly of aluminum.

It was not only the magic of its name that made the Silver Ghost one of the most famous cars ever built. Rolls-Royce went on producing it from 1907 to 1925, for at the time it was introduced it touched the heights of perfection, and even today there are relatively few cars that can match it for silent smoothness.

As can be seen from the 1909 example at Beaulieu, the Silver Ghost is a very large car. It was produced in two versions, one with a 135.5-inch (3,442-mm) wheelbase chassis, and a long version with 143.5-inch (3,645 mm) wheelbase. The engine is of "square" dimensions—114.2-mm bore and stroke—but a slightly larger version was introduced that year with lengthened stroke and a total displacement of 7,428 cc instead of the 7,036 cc as on the Beaulieu car. There are six cylinders in two blocks of three, and side valves. Rolls-Royce never declares the power of its cars, replying "Enough" to those eager for specific figures. It is estimated, however, that the 7-liter engine gave 48 horsepower at 1,250 rpm.

The water-cooled engine is conventional, but a product of the finest craftsmanship; it is pressure-lubricated by a system that increases the flow of oil with pressure on the accelerator. There are two separate ignition systems, by magneto and battery, and there is both automatic and manual control of the carburetor mixture.

A cone clutch is used with a four-speed gearbox having direct drive on third, allowing speeds from 53 mph (5 to 85 kph) in that gear, while the car would hold 62 mph in the overdrive top, averaging about 18 miles per gallon of gasoline.

Suspension is by semi-elliptic leaf springs at the front, and three-quarter elliptic leaves at the rear, with Rolls-Royce's own friction shock absorbers. The wheels are of artillery type with wooden spokes, and tire sizes varied with the chassis; those on the shorter wheelbase model being 875x105 front and 880x120 rear. The footbrake works on the transmission and the handbrake on the rear drums. Countless kinds of bodywork have appeared on the Silver Ghost chassis, whose reputation for superb engineering became worldwide.

Lanchester 25-hp

1912

Except in the British Isles, the name Lanchester is not very well known outside veteran car circles. Yet the Lanchester brothers made a great contribution to the technical side of the motor industry, applying scientific principles in an age characterized by empiricism. What they probably lacked was adequate and understanding business backing to establish their ideas commercially.

The 1912, 25-horsepower Lanchester is itself evidence of their contribution. Capable of 53 mph (85 kph), it was a first-rate product for its day, and one that could stand comparison with a Rolls-Royce. After designing their famous engines with two opposed cylinders and a system of connecting rods that eliminated vibration, Lanchester followed up with this in-line, four-cylinder car. Its "square" engine has a 101.6-mm bore and stroke, giving a capacity of 3,299 cc; the effective power must have been about 35 horsepower at 1,400 rpm, but may have been higher as the engine could rev to 2,000 rpm.

Location of the engine is unusual; it is set back between the cowl and the front seat, so that driver and passenger sat on each side of it, as in a modern forward-control truck or van. The engine is pressure lubricated, has dual ignition by magneto and spark coil, and there is a torsional vibration damper fitted to the front end of the crankshaft. The overhead valves are disposed horizontally, and carburetion is by evaporation, using the famous Lanchester wick carburetor.

The very advanced transmission, with an epicyclic gearbox with three speeds controlled by friction, is very much like a modern automatic transmission, and the power is transmitted to the rear wheels by propeller shaft and underslung worm drive—another Lanchester speciality. The footbrake acts on the transmission by means of a system of multiple plates, while the handbrake acts on the drum brakes on the rear wheels.

Both front and rear suspensions are by cantilever springs, giving an extremely comfortable ride, and the wheels are Rudge-Whitworth wire type, fitted with 880x120 tires. The wheelbase of the shorter version is 115 inches and of the longer one 127 inches, while both wheel tracks measure 58 inches. Weight of the Lanchester 25-horsepower is a substantial 3,500 pounds, allowing a top speed of 53 mph.

It cannot be called handsome, but there are many advanced features in this Lanchester. The four-cylinder overhead valve engine protrudes into the front compartment, as on a modern forward control truck, and the car has a three-speed epicyclic gearbox and underslung worm rear drive.

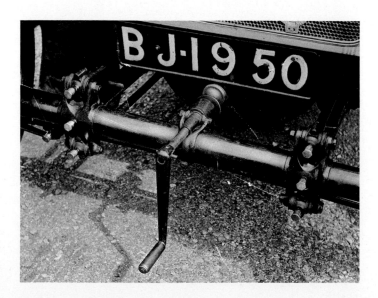

Daimler 30-hp

1913

The British Daimler Company began as licensees of the parent German firm's patents, and in the beginning merely imported cars. Very shortly, however, it became independent, producing high-class cars designed by its own technicians and concentrating on elegant, quiet vehicles, chiefly with closed bodies manufactured by Daimler itself. The large 1913, six-cylinder engine, five-seater saloon to be seen at the museum at Beaulieu was produced in the years immediately before World War I, and its engine makes it one of the more interesting cars of that period.

In view of the difficulties that were encountered in lowering the noise volume of a four-stroke engine with conventional poppet valves, the Daimler Company had, in 1909, acquired a license to develop the American Knight patent for double-sleeve valves. In this system, there are two slim sleeves, between the cylinder and the

piston in each cylinder. They slide up and down, and have ports corresponding to the combustion chamber, which, in its turn, has ports for inlet and exhaust. The two sleeves are moved by a camshaft through short connecting rods, and the system depends on making the ports of the sleeves coincide with the cylinder head ports.

The result is absolutely silent operation by the Knight sleeve-valve engine. Also, experience showed that if the engine was well and accurately manufactured, it would run over a long period of time without giving trouble, even though it produced rather limited power and emitted heavy oil smoke in its exhaust.

The elegant saloon body of this Daimler has no internal division between the driving seat and rear seats, indicating that it was not chauffeur driven. Note the window straps, like those used on trains.

The water-cooled, six-cylinder engine of the 1913 30-horsepower Daimler has a 90x130-mm bore and stroke, a 4,962-cc displacement, dual ignition by high-tension magneto and coil, and a single carburetor. With an effective power that may have been greater than the 60 horsepower declared, this car supposedly could attain 60 mph.

The car has a cone-type clutch and a four-speed gearbox, and final drive is by an open drive shaft and worm gear.

The chassis is traditional, and is suspended by semi-elliptic leaf springs. The wheelbase measures 138.5 inches, and the large-diameter wheels have 920x120 tires. Braking is on the transmission and the rear wheels.

The Prince Henry has been called Laurence Pomeroy's masterpiece. It is a superbly balanced and elegant car, which could manage 75 mph despite a weight of about 2,425 pounds. The runningboard is used to mount a toolbox. The famous Vauxhall flutes on the radiator are continued into that handsome aluminum hood.

Vauxhall Prince Henry

1914

A famous long-distance reliability-cum-speed contest of the heroic age of motoring was the Prince Henry Cup Trial, sponsored by Prince Henry of Prussia and staged in Germany before World War I. This precursor of the modern rally played a great part in developing fast sporting cars in Europe. The British Vauxhall Company entered a team of 3-liter cars in the 1910 event, winning Prince Henry plaques for their performance.

Thus the name Prince Henry was passed to a sporting production model Vauxhall designed by Laurence Pomeroy, of which the 1914 car preserved at Beaulieu's National Motor Museum is a fine example. Its four-cylinder, in-line engine is larger than the original Prince Henry, with a 95x140-mm bore and stroke, giving a 3,969-cc displacement and a power output of 75 horsepower at 2,500 rpm.

The cylinders are cast in a single block, with the head removable. The side valves are in line, operated by a camshaft located in the crankcase. The car has high-tension magneto ignition and a Claudel-Hobson carburetor; cooling is by pump and fan, with pressure lubrication. A Hele-Shaw multiple-disk clutch is used with a four-speed gearbox, driving through a propeller shaft to a 3:1 rear final drive.

The Prince Henry Vauxhall chassis is of conventional type, and the suspension, too, is of normal design for the time, with rigid axles and semi-elliptic leaf springs all around. But it is the precision of the design that stands out—in the weight distribution, in the relative lightness of the unsprung parts, and in the excellent roadholding. Handsome Rudge-Whitworth wire wheels with knock-off hubcaps carry 820x120 tires. The Beaulieu car also carries two spare wheels, one on each side of its elegant four-seater touring bodywork. The finish is superb in red, with a polished aluminum hood, brightly plated sporting headlamps, and the classic Vauxhall radiator.

The brakes on this car are very powerful, but have a short life, requiring adjustment every 300 miles or so if used rigorously. Top speed is given as 75 mph.

127

Morris Cowley Bullnose
1924

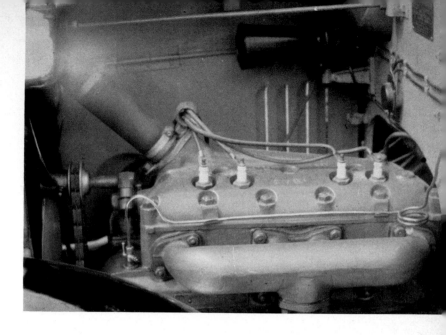

William Richard Morris was, of course, the founder of the famous English make of car bearing his name, which is still going strong today as a member of the British Leyland Motor Corporation. One of the most famous of the countless Morris models built in over 60 years is the Bullnose. Characterized by the rounded radiator, which provided its nickname, it was one of the greatest production successes ever, being manufactured in quantity between 1915 and 1926, then continued for several years subsequently with a flat radiator.

It is not widely known that Morris, in an effort to keep costs down, turned to the American automobile industry for assistance; in the early period up to World War I, engines and various other parts were supplied from the United States. In the classic version of the 1920s, as seen at Beaulieu, however, the Bullnose has a British-made in-line, four-cylinder engine with side valves. Lubrication is of mixed type, with pressure feed for the crankshaft bearings and the camshaft, and splash feed for the connecting rods and pistons.

Cylinder dimensions are 69.5x102 mm, giving a cubic capacity of 1,548 cc. The nominal horsepower by Royal Automobile Club rating is 11.9, and the effective output about 26 horsepower at 2,800 rpm, which corresponds to a fairly modest maximum speed of around 50 mph. The car has magneto ignition and a Zenith horizontal single-barrel carburetor.

Transmission is via a dual-plate clutch and a 3-speed gearbox in unit with the engine; this gearbox, like the engine, shows a certain amount of American influence. Transmission is by an enclosed shaft and a cardan joint on the gearbox, which is protected by a spherical joint. The front axle is suspended by semi-elliptic leaf springs, while at the back a three-quarter elliptic system is employed. Shock absorbers were an optional extra between

1922 and 1924, while the hand and footbrakes worked on the rear wheels only until 1925, when four-wheel brakes were standardized. The Cowley Bullnose played a vital part in W. R. Morris's drastic price reductions, which probably saved the Morris Company from extinction in 1921 when other firms were raising their prices.

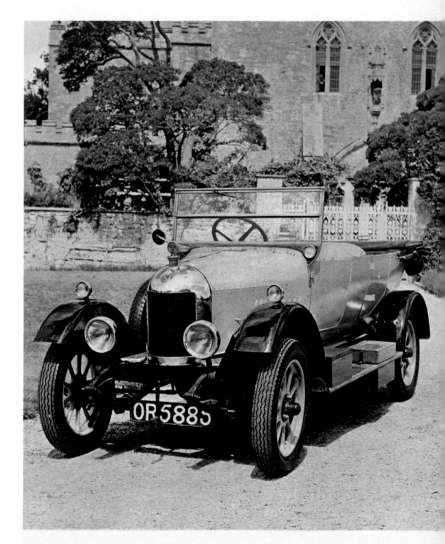

This is one of the great forerunners of the modern runabout. Weighing only 1,650 pounds and capable of 50 mph, the Bullnose was the English "Tin Lizzie," inexpensive, easy to maintain, and dependable.

1000hp Sunbeam

1927

By 1926 Major (later Sir) Henry Segrave had already set up a new absolute land speed record for cars at 152.33 mph in a 4-liter Sunbeam. However, in view of the progress made by his rivals, he felt that to recapture the record he would need a special new car of much greater power—the 1927, 1,000-horsepower machine, which the Sunbeam concern undertook to build.

Louis Coatalen and J. S. Irving, the designers, chose two Sunbeam Matabele V-12 aero-engines, each with a 122x160 mm bore and stroke, and a displacement of 22,444 cc. The maximum power developed by each unit was in the region of 435–445 horsepower at 2,000 rpm, but Coatalen and Segrave agreed on the spectacular figure of 1,000 horsepower for the title. One engine is installed at the front, ahead of the driving seat, and the other behind. The rear engine was first started with compressed air, and then it in turn started up the front engine. Each engine has its own 3-speed gearbox, from which power is transmitted to a cross shaft with sprockets; side chains take the drive to the rear wheels.

The bodywork was boldly unconventional for the time, being all-enveloping; it had been intended to fully enclose the rear wheels with covers, but eventually the car was run without them. The wire wheels carried specially developed Dunlop 35x6-inch tires, and the four-wheel drum brakes were complemented by a Dewandre vacuum assist.

This was one of the new generation of record cars, specially built for the job rather than derived from a racing car, and using an aero-engine to obtain the enormous power required instead of resorting to the trouble and expense of building a special power unit. On March 29, 1927, Major Segrave reached a mean speed of 203.792 mph on Daytona Beach, Florida, breaking Malcolm Campbell's former world record by over 28 mph and exceeding 200 mph on land for the first time—without even using full throttle!

Four tons of ingeniously engineered metal pushed along at over 200 mph—that in brief is Segrave's great twin-engined Sunbeam.

Golden Arrow

1929

When his 1927 land speed record of 203.792 mph was broken, first by Malcolm Campbell and then by the American Ray Keech in his Triplex Special, Major Henry Segrave resolved to regain it with a new car. This was the Irving-Napier Golden Arrow, which is one of the most interesting exhibits at the National Motor Museum at Beaulieu.

Designed by Capt. J. S. Irving, built by the KLG engineering works at Putney, outside London, and driven at Daytona Beach by Segrave, it raised the world record to 231.466 mph in March 1929. The engine, which enabled it to achieve such a speed, is a Napier Lion aircraft unit built for the Schneider Trophy race; this has 12 cylinders in three rows like an inverted broad arrow—that is, with the central row vertical and the other two inclined at 60 degrees.

Bore and stroke are 139.7x130.2 mm, giving a total engine capacity of 23,948 cc and a maximum power of 925 horsepower at 3,300 rpm. The crankshaft rotates on six roller bearings, and there is a main connecting rod with two articulated rods for each group of cylinders, four valves per cylinder with two overhead camshafts, a three-barrel carburetor, and dual magneto ignition.

The transmission is unusual; there is a dry multi-plate clutch with vacuum servo control, a 3-speed gearbox, which is separate from the engine, and twin propeller shafts without differentials to the rear driving wheels. This arrangement permits a low driving seat between the two drive shafts. Suspension is by semi-elliptic leaf springs all around, with friction dampers, and there are drum brakes to all four wheels with steel shoes and vacuum-assisted operation.

The striking streamlining of the Golden Arrow conforms closely with the three-bank engine, while between the wheels are high fairings that house flush aircraft-type surface radiators. To reinforce this system, an inside tank is packed with ice. The long, tapering tail embodies a vertical stabilizing fin, with the driver's head fairing merging into it.

Golden Arrow was very sturdily constructed, and the overall weight is close to 3.5 tons. The wire-spoked wheels carry light alloy disks and special treadless tires, which were developed by Dunlop for the record attempt. These had a guaranteed life at record-breaking speeds of 25 seconds. The tires to be seen today on the car at Beaulieu are non-original, having heavy treads.

The remarkable shape of this record car is built around its inverted "broad arrow" Napier Lion engine, straight out of a racing airplane.

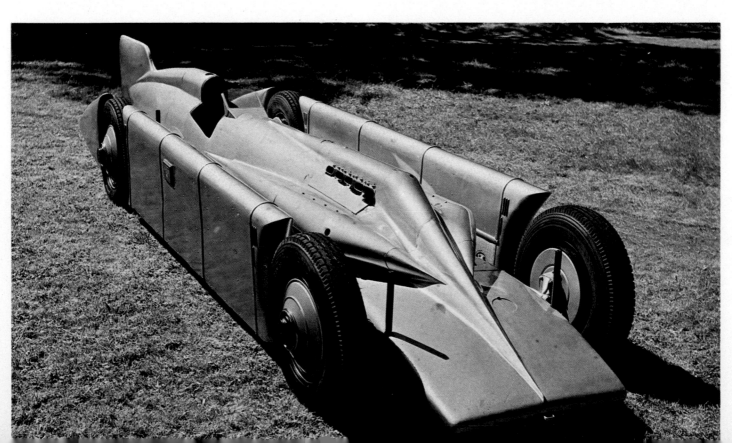

Bentley 4.5-liter
1928

Probably no make more aptly epitomizes the classic vintage sports car than the Bentley. Walter Owen Bentley was a great designer, and in quality of construction and design, if not luxury, his make is a worthy rival to the equally famous Rolls-Royce. During their lamentably short production life from 1921 to 1931, Bentley cars signified speed with rugged reliability, as emphasized by their five fictories in the Le Mans 24-Hour Race in 1924, 1927, 1928, 1929, and 1930, and in other long-distance events.

The 1928 4.5-liter, four-seater tourer at the Beaulieu National Motor Museum is a well-restored specimen of the model developed to replace the older 3-liter car. It has a very sturdy in-line, four-cylinder engine, with a 100x140-mm bore and stroke, and a total displacement of 4,398 cc. There are four valves to each cylinder, which are operated by a single overhead camshaft driven by vertical shaft. Ignition is by two magnetos with synchronized variable advance and two spark plugs per cylinder. Large twin SU carburetors are fitted, lubrication is on the dry sump system, and cooling is by pump circulation controlled by a thermostat, in conjunction with the handsome vee radiator. The clutch is of cone type, and the separate gearbox has four forward speeds. Suspension is by semi-elliptic leaf springs all around, which are damped by friction shock absorbers. Mechanical braking is on all four wheels. Wheelbase of the normal 4.5-liter Bentley is 130 inches (there were eight special shorter models). Dunlop 5.25x21 tires are fitted to the Rudge-Whitworth wire wheels. These are always an imposing feature with their "knock-off" quick-release hubcaps.

The 4.5-liter Bentley appeared in diverse open and closed forms, and many are still to be seen in action today. Bentley cars are remarkable for their longevity, and of the 3,061 built during the lifetime of the make, well over 1,000 survive today, driven by enthusiastic owners who mostly belong to the Bentley Drivers' Club, one of Britain's most thriving one-make organizations.

Here is a car that cannot be imagined in any color but British racing green. W. O. Bentley had in greater measure than most the gift of creating engines that were not only powerful but also things of beauty. Note the arrangement of the carburetors, and that camshaft cover.

E.R.A. B-type
1935

The letters E.R.A., which stand for English Racing Automobiles, were chosen by Raymond Mays, Peter Berthon, and Humphrey Cook to denote the cars built by them at Bourne, Lincolnshire, when, in 1934, they decided to try and reestablish Britain's waning name in

international motor racing. The remarkable aspect of their achievement is that they managed to build such excellent cars, competing with much honor in this tough field, despite the simplest of means.

The engine of the E.R.A. was derived from a normal Riley six-cylinder production power unit, and the racing unit was built in three different engine capacities—1,100, 1,500, and 2,000 cc. Romulus, the E.R.A. illustrated here, which is an attraction at the new National Motor Museum, is one of the 1,500-cc cars built in 1935-36 for the *voiturette* class of international racing. It was raced with very great success by B. Bira (Prince Birabongse of Siam), who scored over a dozen victories with it.

The in-line, six-cylinder engine has a cast-iron cylinder block-cum-crankcase and an aluminum head. Bore and stroke are 57.5x95.2 mm, giving a displacement of 1,488 cc. A special three-bearing crankshaft is fitted, which is able to withstand the power output of around 150 horsepower at up to 7,000 rpm. Overhead valves are operated by two camshafts placed high in the crankcase and connected by short pushrods and rockers; this ar-

rangement avoids the complication of twin overhead camshafts. A Murray Jamieson supercharger of the Roots type is mounted vertically and driven off the front of the crankshaft, drawing air through a single SU carburetor.

Transmission of the E.R.A. racing car is unusual in that it incorporates an Armstrong Siddeley Wilson epicyclic four-speed gearbox with a pre-selector operated by a lever close to the steering wheel. Although this gearbox is heavy, it enables the driver to pre-select his gears well before a corner and to keep his hands on the wheel.

Suspension on the A and B type E.R.A.s is of the old-fashioned type, with rigid axles and semi-elliptic leaf springing. Friction-type shock absorbers were originally employed, but in many cases were replaced by hydraulic units. Hydraulically operated brakes with large-diameter drums are fitted to Bira's car, but mechanical-type brakes were originally used.

Jaguar D-type

1954

The impressive-looking D-type Jaguar launched in 1954 for international sports car racing is a derivative of the earlier XK120C type, which by then had already won widespread fame for its makers. The car on display at the National Motor Museum was the first to be built, and it ran as a works car in the dramatic 1954 Le Mans 24-Hour Race, when Rolt and Hamilton in a D-type placed a close second to a larger-engined Ferrari. But D Jaguars won at Le Mans for the next three years, at speeds of 106.99, 104.46, and 113.85 mph.

The water-cooled engine, with twin overhead camshafts, cast-iron block, and aluminum head and crankcase, is the classic Jaguar in-line, six-cylinder. The cylinders have an 83x106-mm bore and stroke, giving an engine capacity of 3,442 cc. Power output is about 240 horsepower at 5,750 rpm, using triple Weber 45 DCO horizontal twin-choke carburetors and coil ignition.

Transmission is by a dry-plate clutch and four-speed gearbox, with synchronization on all but the bottom gear. The chassis is very advanced, having a full monocoque center section, with square-section steel tube subframe to support the engine and front suspension, and a separate tail structure that contains the fuel tank and spare wheel. Independent front suspension by wishbones and torsion bars is employed, while at the rear the rigid axle is suspended by radius arms and torsion bars.

As is well known, Jaguar was the first to use disk brakes in long-distance racing (it used Dunlop brakes), and this gave the cars a marked advantage over their rivals. On the D-type the light alloy disk wheels and the 6.50x16 tires are also made by Dunlop. The all-enveloping bodywork is beautifully formed and is highly aerodynamically efficient, as was proved at Le Mans where they habitually outstripped more powerful cars and had a maximum speed of over 170 mph. The integral tail fin, which merges so gracefully with the rest of the body, is a D-type characteristic. The first cars were built of magnesium alloy, which saved on weight and enhanced the performance, but subsequently aluminum alloy was used. Wheelbase of the car is 90 inches.

The beautiful curves of the bodywork are typical of the Jaguar D-type and inspired other designers. Note the easy accessibility of the engine thanks to the way the whole front bodywork swings up. The car weighed less than 1,765 pounds dry and had a maximum speed of over 170 mph.

SCIENCE MUSEUM

A proposal to form a museum of science in London was first made shortly after the Great Exhibition of 1851 by Albert, the Prince Consort. Six years later the first collection, comprising foodstuffs, animal products, manufactured articles and building materials, as well as educational apparatus, was opened in South Kensington. A collection of scientific apparatus was begun in 1874 and greatly enlarged in 1876, when apparatus lent by other museums, much of it later purchased, was placed on exhibition.

Further additions in 1884, 1900, and 1903 swelled the size of the collections, and in 1909 it was decided to separate the pure and applied arts from the scientific. Thus the Victoria and Albert Museum was opened for the former, and the new Science Museum on the other side of Exhibition Road was opened to house the latter. Here many important historical motoring exhibits are displayed. The aim of the museum is to promote the study of technical developments and to illustrate the application of physical science to technical industry. This is effected by the comprehensive display of objects, diagrams, and photos, so that they trace development of a particular subject from its very beginnings to modern times.

To help the student of history, there is a descriptive catalog listing the material at the museum for each section, since lack of space prevents everything from being displayed. These catalogs are among the finest of their kind published. Other handbooks and monographs deal with the historic evolution of specific branches of science.

On the subject of cars, for example, there is a very useful catalog of vehicles, engines, accessories, and so forth, and a history of the evolution of the utility car. The list includes no less than 478 items. Only a portion of them are actual cars, of course, but it is this wealth of separate contributory components that makes the collection more interesting, since it is far simpler to trace the evolution of a subject through its different phases.

There are innumerable photographs, drawings, and well-constructed models of many important forerunners of the motor car. They include diagrams of the 1807 de Rivaz, the world's first carriage to be powered by an internal combustion engine, literally an "explosion" engine; Sam Brown's vacuum gas-engined carriage of 18 ; Lenoir's vehicle of 1862; and the Delamarre-Debouteville, built in Rouen in 1883. Siegfried Marcus' gasoline-driven car, which is alleged to have been built 1875, is shown in model form. The earliest actual car on display is an 1888 Benz.

Altogether there are about fifty fine motor cars to be examined. Most are British veteran or vintage models, but among later cars of interest is the Rover gas turbine car of 1950. The post-World War II era is also represented by examples of Ford cars, the tiny three-wheeled Bond Minicar, and many superb scale models. Nor can one forget the counterattractions of subjects other than cars in such a rich museum.

Lanchester 8hp Phaeton

1897

The early cars made by the Lanchester brothers were designed by Frederick, who was one of the finest British automobile engineers of all time. The 1897 Phaeton displayed at the Science Museum is exceptionally interesting from a technical point of view, with features far in advance of contemporary design, in particular its air-cooled engine with two horizontally opposed cylinders.

In order to obtain perfect balance of the moving parts, two balanced crankshafts, each with its own fly-wheel, are set centrally in the engine, rotating in opposite directions through helical gearing. Each of the two pistons has three connecting rods, two of them coupled to one crankshaft and one to the other. In this way the forces of inertia cancel each other out, and the engine is completely free of vibration. It was also exceptionally quiet for the time and free from many of the troubles that afflicted early engines.

The Science Museum lists a 5 inx4.5-in (127x114.3-mm) bore and stroke with a 2,896-cc displacement, but a book devoted to the history of the Lanchesters gives the bore and stroke as 127x137 mm and the capacity as 3,471 cc. In both cases the power is indicated as 8 horsepower at 700–800 rpm, but reaching 10 horsepower at 1,200 rpm. By ingenious use of a disk valve, one large valve to each cylinder serves to pass incoming gas and burnt exhaust. The air cooling is by forced draft from a flywheel-driven fan; carburetion is by the simple but effective Lanchester wick system; and low-tension ignition is provided by perhaps the first flywheel magneto in the history of the automobile.

A further advanced feature is fully automatic lubrication; transmission of this remarkable car is by an epicyclic two-speed gearbox, and the clutch is arranged in such

a way that it also serves as a brake, applying the driven plate on the back of the cone. Yet another feature ahead of its time is a propeller shaft (instead of chains) to a worm-drive live rear axle.

The chassis is formed of steel tubes, and the front axle has cantilever springing; the rear axle has no springs but, instead, the body itself is sprung at four points. "Side lever" tiller-type steering is used; the wheelbase is 70 inches and the track 46 inches. The wire wheels carry 36x2.5 in pneumatic tires. This unique 19th-century car could maintain a speed of over 20 mph.

A feature of this car is the leather front fender with metal struts; it could be hinged forward to give passengers easier access. Typically Lanchester was the tiller steering, set to the right of the driving seat. Beneath this car's erect and homely exterior much ingenious mechanism was concealed, including the silent, horizontally opposed twin-cylinder engine, epicyclic transmission, and drive shaft.

Daimler 12-hp

1898

The 1898 Daimler wagonette, which originally belonged to the Hon. John Scott-Montagu, later the second Lord Montagu of Beaulieu, and is now at the Science Museum in London, is the first four-cylinder model built by the Daimler Motor Company Ltd. of Coventry. This firm originated as an agency for selling Daimler's patents in England, but later became completely independent of the German parent concern and their designs.

Practically from the start, British-built Daimlers differed from their German counterparts. The front-mounted, water-cooled, in-line engine has four vertical cylinders cast in pairs, with an 89.9x119.9-mm bore and stroke, and a power output of 12 horsepower at 700 rpm. Lubrication of this engine is by drip feed to the bearings via sight feeds on the dash, and by splash from the crankshaft to the cylinders and other moving parts.

The inlet valves are automatically operated (by suction), while the exhaust valves are actuated by an external camshaft on the nearside of the engine. Speed is controlled by a governor through a hit-and-miss gear. The car has Simms-Bosch low-tension magneto ignition in its present form, but was originally fitted with hot tube ignition. A spray-type carburetor is fitted, and the cooling water is circulated by a pump through the radiator, which is mounted low at the front of the car.

The leather-faced cone-type clutch of this Daimler is interesting; it can be controlled either by the clutch pedal or through the pedal and lever, which control the two braking systems (on the crossshaft of the transmission and on the rear wheels). In this way not even an inexperienced driver could stall the engine by mistake. The four-speed gearbox is of the straight-through type, is separate from the engine, being connected by short shaft, and embodies a differential and crossshaft from which the final drive is by side chains. Reversing on this car is effected by a separate lever that slides three bevel wheels. The final drive chains are partially covered.

The chassis is of armored wood with steel side plates, and the suspension shackles and cross members are bolted in place. Suspension is by semi-elliptic leaf springs to the front and rear axles. The steering looks surprisingly modern with its steering wheel at a time when tiller control was still common. The wooden-spoked wheels are of unequal size, those at the front being 28 inches in diameter, and at the rear 38 inches; all four have solid rubber tires. The wheelbase of this Daimler measures 79 inches.

The English 12-hp Daimler weighs about 3,300 pounds and could travel at 25 mph. It was a sturdy car, as reliable as any in its day, even if the solid rubber tires could not have added to the comfort of the ride.

Morgan Cyclecar
1914

The cyclecar, and in particular the three-wheeler version, became an anomaly in an age when giants prospered; it was an attempt to make the motor vehicle popular by means of lower costs and smaller fuel consumption. The Englishman H. F. S. Morgan is the first manufacturer to come to mind in this field, largely because his

make outlasted all the others and today has its own particular niche in the four-wheeled market.

The vehicle exhibited at the Science Museum is one of the earliest Morgan three-wheelers, for the make began in 1910 with single- and twin-cylinder, single-seater models. This 1914 Cyclecar has a front-mounted, air-cooled, vee-twin, side-valve J.A.P. engine with cylinders at 45 degrees; its bore and stroke are 85.5x85 mm, giving a total displacement of 976 cc. It has pressure lubrication and ignition by magneto.

The power of the normal production Runabout was 8 horsepower, but special high-performance versions with overhead valve engines were developed that were capable of reaching remarkably high speeds. Morgan himself covered nearly 60 miles in one hour while successfully attacking 1,100-cc class records at Brooklands in 1912.

The transmission is interesting: a flywheel clutch and propeller shaft transmit power to a cross shaft that carries two chain sprockets of different sizes. The cross shaft is splined and carries two dog clutches, which are operated by the gear lever; these engage one or other of the sprockets, which drive the single rear wheel by separate side chains, thus giving a choice of two speeds.

The chassis consists of a single, large-diameter tube, to which are attached the front engine mounting and front suspension assembly. This suspension anticipated by several years the sliding pillar independent system used on the Lancia Lambda, wherein the pillars, with concentric coil springs, also function as steering pins. It was simple, ingenious, and effective and survives to this day on the Morgan car. Rear suspension on the Cyclecar is by two cantilever springs; the wire wheels have 700x80 tires; and two people were accommodated in rudimentary comfort.

The lines of the Morgan three-wheeler are unique. The example shown here is a very old model, but more recent ones can still be seen in use on English roads. The classic J.A.P. motorcycle engine drives alternative sets of chains and sprockets, giving two speeds. This two-seater weighed only about 670 pounds and could manage a speed of 44 mph.

MUSEO DELL'AUTOMOBILE CARLO BISCARETTI DI RUFIA

On the banks of the Po River, facing the Turin hills, there stands a very modern building with a long curved façade—the Carlo Biscaretti di Ruffia automobile museum, which was built with the assistance of the city of Turin, which is the cradle of the Italian motor industry.

The name of this museum is a tribute to the man who, more than any other, recorded the history of the motor car in Italy; he dedicated his whole life to it, with his work as an artist and historian, and a good part of his means. From the 1930s onward, Count Biscaretti gathered together old cars, which form the basis of the present-day collection; he did this because he felt that old and unusable cars should be kept for future generations.

It was often an arduous battle that this son of a pioneer of Italian motor car manufacture (his father was a co-founder of FIAT with Agnelli and others) had to wage against the unappreciative majority of the times, especially when the collection, which he had so laboriously gathered together, was partially broken up because of World War II.

Then at last things brightened up. In 1957 Biscaretti wrote, "Today, at last, after 25 years of waiting, the dream of my life is becoming a reality." In fact, the organization that was to give Turin its car museum had been set up. The building was inaugurated in November 1960, but sadly, the man who inspired its creation had died a short time before and was denied the joy of seeing it completed.

The elegant building bearing his name is without doubt the most beautiful car museum in existence. It covers an area of about 14,000 square yards, of which some 6,000 are covered by the building itself, while the rest consists of gardens and parking areas. About 200 cars are on show, as well as separate parts, accessories, special sections devoted to tires, gasoline, rubber, coachwork, motor racing, and other items of interest.

The blend of new building and old cars is a great success, thanks largely to the skills of the chief architect, Amedeo Albertini, and his special feeling for matters concerning wheeled vehicles. The museum includes rooms for meetings and films, a fitted laboratory for renovation work, and a section for technical and historical documentation, where there is in progress one of the most complete research programs ever known in the history of the motor car.

The collections are arranged systematically. The main floor houses most of the production-line cars, principally Italian, the chassis, and an interesting model collection of vehicles that preceded the horse-less carriage. These models were made by Count Biscaretti himself. The first floor contains, in two galleries, priceless examples of early cars from 1893 to 1905 and 1905 to 1910, while the second floor takes the form of a vast balcony overlooking the main hall below. It contains sports and racing cars, a small but important selection of motorcycles and bicycles, and a technical section for chassis and accessories.

The museum contains several cars of unique historical value, like the Itala, which won the legendary Peking–Paris race in 1907; the FIAT, which won the French Grand Prix the same year; and other famous racing cars such as Lancia, Alfa Romeo, Ferrari, Maserati, Mercedes, the first turbine powered FIAT, and the humble but equally legendary FIAT 18BL lorry, which carried the Italian army in World War I.

Many of the road cars are in working order, and they regularly take part in vintage or veteran motoring events. The collection is always being augmented by "new" rare Italian and foreign cars, since the museum authorities consider it necessary to buy these as they come to light. It need hardly be said that only one person could preside over this museum with the same loving care as its founder, and that is his son, Rodolfo Biscaretti di Ruffia.

Peugeot Quadricycle
1894

This intriguing little car is one of the earliest models produced by the famous old French concern of Peugeot Frères of Valentigny. It is, in fact, the third type they produced, and is called a Quadricycle, although in design it constitutes a real motor car, if one of modest power and dimensions.

The engine is the classic Daimler narrow-angle vee twin-cylinder, which was supplied to Peugeot by Panhard-Levassor, who were French licensees for the engine. It has a bore and stroke of 60x100 mm, giving it a modest total cylinder capacity of 565 cc, and a power output of about 2.5 horsepower at 1,000 rpm. The engine is mounted between the seats and the rear axle and has platinum tube—that is, "hot tube"—ignition, a spray-type carburetor, "drip" lubrication, and water cooling.

The power is transmitted from the engine through a leather cone clutch to a chain of gears that gives four forward speeds and a reverse, and then to a countershaft with differential carrying chain sprockets on each side. From there side chains pass the drive to the rear wheels. Reverse is obtained by operating a handle situated to the right of the seat. Braking is on the transmission only.

The steering is typical of early Peugeots; that is, it has a vertical column with a form of double handlebar instead of the usual tiller. There is a sprocket at the bottom of the steering column, with a chain connecting it to a larger sprocket just behind the front axle, which operates the drag links to move the wheels.

The chassis is a neat construction of brazed tubes, clearly derived from bicycle practice, which is not surprising since Peugeot was also a cycle manufacturer. A novelty, however, is the use of the frame tubes to carry the cooling water for the engine. Suspension of the little 2.5 horsepower Peugeot is by a single transverse leaf spring at the front, and by semi-elliptics at the rear.

Sturdy wire-spoked wheels are fitted, carrying solid rubber tires. The wheelbase is 64 inches and track 45 inches. The four-seater body is of "vis-à-vis" type, with front and rear seats facing each other.

This neat little Peugeot "vis-à-vis" weighs about 1,100 pounds and would reach 11 mph. A two-cylinder Daimler engine was used.

146

FIAT
3.5-hp
1899

The first FIAT model is particularly interesting, both because it represents the starting point of an automobile manufacturing company that was to become one of biggest in the world, and because, in contrast with many other early designs, it was not the result of the pioneering work of a single person, but from the outset the product of a real factory.

FIAT was founded in 1899 by a group of Piedmontese gentlemen (the initials signify Fabbrica Italiana Automobili Torino), and from the beginning it was run as a proper organization. Evidence of this is the man who planned the first FIAT car, the engineer Aristide Faccioli; he took careful account of what had already been done elsewhere, weighed up the pros and cons, and worked out a design for a small car, which proved successful almost from the start.

The example at the Biscaretti museum is one of

This is one of only three examples of the earliest two-cylinder rear-engined FIAT models to survive, and it is in perfect condition. Note the tubular radiator and the vast top—with that erected the car's 16 mph maximum must have been difficult to attain.

about twenty built in 1899. It has a rear-mounted, horizontal twin-cylinder engine with water cooling by means of a front radiator. Dimensions of the two cylinders are 65-mm bore and 99-mm stroke, giving it a total capacity of 679 cc. The effective power output was around 4 horsepower, but for fiscal reasons the model was called the 3.5-horsepower. The engine could turn at up to 1,000 rpm, and has automatic inlet valves. Its electrical ignition is by trembler coil and battery.

Transmission from the engine is through a leather cone-type clutch and a sliding type 3-speed gearbox with no reverse, driving a countershaft incorporating the differential, with final drive by side chains to the rear wheels. There are two contracting band brakes: one pedal-operated and acting on the transmission, the other a handbrake operating on the rear wheels.

The car at the Biscaretti museum has wooden-

spoked wheels, but wire wheels were optional on this model. The tires are 580x55 mm at the front and 670x55 mm at the rear. Steering is by means of a vertical column and double handlebar similar to that used on early Peugeots. The frame is of armored wood, and both axles are suspended. At the front the springs are fully elliptic, while those at the rear are semi-elliptic.

Like all small cars of the period, the FIAT is extremely compact, with a wheelbase of only 58 inches. The body is a four-seater "vis-à-vis," or face-to-face, and is equipped with a notably voluminous top.

Darracq 9.5-hp

1902

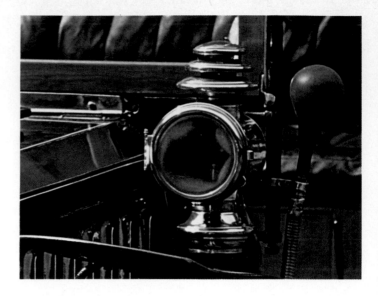

The French-built Darracq was one of the first cars to go into quantity production, and it was sold in thousands at a very reasonable price. The 9.5-horsepower single-cylinder model of 1902, on exhibit at the Biscaretti museum, was derived from the 6.5-horsepower model of the previous year. It has a bore and stroke of 112x130 mm, with a capacity of 1,281 cc, which is large for a sin-

Thanks to its tubular chassis, this Darracq is a light car, scaling about 1,320 pounds, and was fast for its day, with a maximum of over 25 mph.

gle cylinder. Power output is 9 horsepower at 1,200 rpm.

The cylinder is of cast iron, bolted to a wide aluminum sump, which also acts as a crosspiece for the frame. The inlet valve is the automatic (suction) type, but has a lever providing variable lift to control running of the engine. The exhaust valve is mechanically operated by normal cam and tappets. The carburetor, situated low down on the right of the engine, takes in pre-heated air through a tube passing close to the exhaust system.

Ignition is by magneto, driven together with the water pump by gears on the front end of the engine. Cooling is by water, with the tubular radiator slung low at the front between the suspension pickups. An "alligator" type hood closely following the Renault type is a characteristic of the early Darracqs. Engine lubrication is of the splash type.

A leather cone-type clutch transmits the drive to a separate gearbox, which has three forward speeds and reverse. The gears are engaged by means of a horizontal lever mounted on the steering column—an early version of the car is its high-geared and, therefore, very heavy verse is engaged by manipulating a lever situated to the right of the driver's seat.

Like Louis Renault, Alexandre Darracq, proprietor of the firm bearing his name, did not like chain drive, and the 9.5-horsepower model has propeller shaft final drive, which is neater, cleaner, and quieter. An adverse feature of the car is its high-geared and, therefore, very heavy steering. The chassis is built of small-diameter steel tubing, and suspension is by semi-elliptic leaf springs at front and rear. The wheelbase measures 71.5 inches front track is 47 inches and rear track 48 inches. The weight of about 1,320 pounds gave this Darracq a lively performance for its time, with a speed of over 25 mph.

The car has wooden artillery-type wheels, wearing 815x105 mm tires at the rear and 760x90 mm at the front. The four-seater open body is distinguished by its tall fringed canopy and the four imposing brass lamps.

Grand Prix FIAT

1907

The year 1907 was an important one for Italian motor racing. Not only was an Itala successful in the Peking–Paris endurance race, but also FIAT scored an unprecedented series of victories with Felice Nazarro at the wheel in the most prestigious races of the day—the Tar-

ga Florio in Sicily, the Kaiserpreis in Germany, and the French Grand Prix. When one remembers that a different car had to be prepared for each of these events, the effort in which the still young FIAT company was involved becomes more significant.

The magnificent car to be seen at the Biscaretti museum is one of the three Grand Prix FIATs built for the race; it is claimed to be the actual example with which Nazzaro won, averaging 70.61 mph in a 477.5-mile contest lasting nearly seven hours. Its mighty in-line engine, in two blocks of two cylinders, measures 180-mm bore x 160-mm stroke, giving each cylinder a capacity of over 4 liters and a total displacement of 16,286 cc!

With a compression ratio of about 4:1, this engine developed 130 horsepower at 1,600 rpm. Its most interesting feature is the valve gear. The valves are overhead in a hemispherical head, which is angled at 60 degrees and operated through pushrods and enormous rocker arms by a single camshaft in the crankcase. A single vertical carburetor and low-tension magneto ignition are employed, and the engine is water-cooled by pump and that massive brass radiator.

Power is transmitted by a multiple-disk-type clutch

The powerful 16.2-liter, 130-horsepower FIAT that won the 1907 French Grand Prix at Dieppe, seen posed in front of the Biscaretti museum at the foot of the monument to the motorized soldier. Note the extensive drilling on hand levers, sprockets, and steering arm to reduce weight.

in an oil bath, and by a short drive shaft, to the four-speed gearbox and transmission crossshaft, which incorporates the differential. Sprockets on each side transmit the drive through side chains to the rear axle. Although it looks surprisingly slender with its shallow pressed-steel side members, the chassis is well braced, with reinforcement from the rigid mounting of the engine and gearbox. Both front and rear axles are suspended by semi-elliptic leaf springs, assisted by a type of embryonic friction shock absorber that was first employed on racing cars to check spring rebound.

Dimensionally it seems a large car, with a wheelbase of 111 inches and tracks of 53 inches, but these measurements are not excessive considering the size of the FIAT's engine. There is room for the engine, the driver's and mechanic's seats, and the rear fuel tank only on F-2, the car bearing this number as it was the one allotted to Nazzaro for the race.

The wooden-spoked wheels have detachable rims for speedy tire changing and are fitted with 875x105-mm tires at the front and 820x120-mm at the rear. The laden weight was estimated at 3,100 pounds, and the car had an estimated maximum speed of 99 mph.

Itala 40-hp Peking-Paris Car

1907

The legendary car that won the unique Peking to Paris endurance race across Asia, traveling via Mongolia to Moscow, Leningrad, and Eastern Europe in 1907, was basically a reinforced production-line 35/40 Itala model. The modifications introduced to equip car and crew for the long, difficult journey did not change its essential characteristics, as can be seen at the Biscaretti museum today, where the actual car driven by Prince Sci-

springs are fitted at front and rear, and the brakes work on the rear wheels only, this applying to the handbrake and the pedal.

The wheels are of the wooden-spoked artillery type; those at the front have detachable rims as presented at the Biscaretti museum, although they are not apparent in pictures taken in 1907. The wheels are fitted with 935x135-mm tires, and a special exhibit at the museum preserves the famous wheel made by a Russian *moujik* when the Itala broke one of its own wheels in an accident.

Instead of full-width rear seats, the car carries two vast tanks, which held an extra 60 gallons of gas to cope with the vast distances of the "race"; the Itala had a range of more than 625 miles without refueling. There are also auxiliary oil and water tanks, each of 50 liters (13 gallons), a big box for tools and spare parts, and a spare set of tires. The third member of the crew sat in a seat between the two side gas tanks. The wheelbase measures 130 inches, and the tracks are 56 inches front and 55.7 inches rear. Its weight, fully laden, was 4,920 pounds, and it could reach a speed of about 44 mph.

pione Borghese and crew is a much prized exhibit.

It has a sturdy water-cooled, four-cylinder engine cast in two blocks of two, with a 130-mm bore and 140-mm stroke, giving an overall capacity of 7,433 cc. Side valves are operated by a camshaft located in the crankcase, and lubrication is a combination of the "splash" and drip-feed systems. Strength and simplicity are essentials of this engine, which produces about 45 horsepower at 1,500 rpm. A multiple-disk clutch transmits the drive through a short drive shaft to the separate four-speed gearbox, and thereafter via a universally jointed propeller shaft to the rear axle. There were doubts at the time as to the suitability of this form of drive over the more primitive but strong side chains, but the brilliant performance of the Itala did much to swing dissenting manufacturers over to shaft drive.

Prince Borghese had the chassis made specially from toughened girder steel, but it followed the production pattern and was stoutly cross-braced. Semi-elliptic leaf

On the wall behind this historic Itala are photographs illustrating the arduous crossing of Asia and Europe by the three-man crew of Borghese, Barzini, and Guizzardi. This sturdy car could travel at 44 mph fully loaded, and often reached its top speed on the steppes.

FIAL Legnano Type A

1908

Not to be confused with FIAT, the FIAL (Fabbrica Italiana Automobili Leganesi) Company of Milan built the Legnano light car between 1906 and 1909. An example survives at the Biscaretti museum for examination. Termed a 6–8 horsepower according to the formula used by the fiscal authority of the time, the Model A was a handy and maneuverable little car, which was distinguished by its perfectly round brass radiator. It has a front-mounted vertical twin-cylinder engine of 85x100-mm bore and stroke, giving it an overall capacity of 1,135 cc and an output of 8 horsepower at 1,100 rpm. The single block is of cast iron, and side valves are employed, actuated by a camshaft housed in the crankcase. The high-tension magneto is also driven off the end of this camshaft via a gear cluster.

Thermosiphon cooling is used, with a four-bladed fan driven by an endless steel spring that functions like a belt. Unlike most cars of the period, the Legnano has a long, steeply sloping steering column, upon which are the hand ignition and carburetor controls.

A leather cone-type clutch takes the drive to a gearbox with three forward speeds and reverse; final drive is by means of a drive shaft. There is nothing unusual about the chassis, which has conventional pressed-steel side members and slender semi-elliptic leaf springs at front and rear. Of interest, however, is the tubular front axle, which has spherical joints for the steering of the front wheels instead of kingpins.

The brakes work on the transmission and the rear wheels; the handbrake connects with small drums on the wheels and the pedal with a drum behind the gearbox. This neat little Legnano two-seater spider has a wheelbase of 78 inches and tracks of 42.5 inches. Tires of 700x80 mm dimensions are worn on wooden-spoked artillery wheels. There is a big toolbox on the running-board, the gas tank is housed under the seat, while at the rear is a kind of lockable trunk. The car weighed only 930 pounds and had a top speed of just 25 mph.

One of the little Italian runabouts of the first decade of this century, the Legnano's round radiator made it an easily recognizable car.

Brixia-Züst 10-hp

1909

The firm of Brixia-Züst was founded in 1902 by a Swiss engineer named Roberto Züst, who settled in Brescia, Italy. Eventually the Züst became the OM, which itself was finally absorbed by FIAT. As the years passed, the factory, which first produced private cars of the touring type, switched to sportier models, and then to trucks and buses, still manufactured today under the name OM.

The neat little 10-horsepower Brixia-Züst on display in the Carlo Biscaretti museum is unusual in that it has one of the few in-line, three-cylinder engines ever used in

a motor car. The two-stroke DKW and Wartburg are subsequent examples, of course, but these differ very much from the Züst unit. This is a very compact monobloc, with fixed head and aluminum crankcase. The head is of the T-type, with lateral valves on both sides of the engine, and is operated by twin camshafts in the crankcase.

A gear group on the exhaust side of the engine drives the Eisermann magneto and water pump, while the oil pump is driven by a vertical shaft, with the oil tank above it, which is provided with a "peephole" to check the oil level. Water cooling is employed with a honeycomb radiator. Bore and stroke are 70x120 mm, giving the three-cylinder engine an overall capacity of 1,495 cc, and an output of 10 horsepower at 1,000 rpm.

This car, which was the ancestor of the OM, has an unusual in-line, three-cylinder engine. It is fairly large and roomy, though the engine is not very powerful, and it could just manage a 30 mph maximum.

This is in many ways a large car in miniature, with seating capacity for four or five people, and with a chassis weight of 1,550 pounds (probably between 1,900–2,100 pounds with body and equipment). It was not a brisk performer, having a maximum speed of 30 mph.

Its 10-brake horsepower was transmitted through a multiple-disk clutch to a separate gearbox which included three forward speeds and a reverse that was engaged by means of a safety lever. Behind the gearbox is a transmission brake with large-diameter drum; final drive is by drive shaft to the live rear axle.

The suspension is by semi-elliptic leaf springs at the front and by three-quarter elliptics at the rear. The chassis side members are pressed steel, dropped in the center to give a lower build, and cross-braced by channel-section members. The wheelbase is 99 inches, and the tracks are 51 inches at the front and 52 inches at the back. Braking is on the transmission and by handbrake on the rear wheels. All the wheels are of wooden artillery type, carrying very thin section pneumatic tires. There is an acetylene lighting system, powered by a gas generator mounted on the offside runningboard.

This was a well-engineered and soundly constructed car with a good reputation for dependability, as befits the product of a conscientious Swiss engineer. The example in the museum is superbly restored.

Adler K 7/15 hp

1912

The German firm of Adler, which first made bicycles, and is today famous for its precision typewriters, manufactured cars between 1900 and 1939. The K7 was first introduced in 1910, but in its 1912 15-horsepower version, as seen at the Biscaretti museum, it has a bigger engine and longer wheelcase.

It has a front-mounted, in-line, four-cylinder engine, cast in iron in two blocks of twin cylinders, with fixed heads and an aluminum crankcase. This crankcase extends rearward to enclose the clutch and the three-speed gearbox, although this is actually separate from the engine, which is connected by a very short shaft. Bore and stroke of the engine are 75x103 mm, giving 1,768 cc, and power output is 17 horsepower at 1,400 rpm.

The K7/15 has a two-bearing crankshaft and parallel side-by-side valves, operated by a camshaft housed in the crankcase. A right-angled take-off from the front end of the camshaft drives the water pump and a magneto of Bosch or Eisemann manufacture. Adler, in fact, used double ignition; there was also a battery and trembler coil system, and twin plugs to each cylinder.

The Adler firm was very late in adopting the pedal accelerator, and this model has the throttle control on the steering wheel hub. The gear lever is inside the body, however, while the handbrake lever remains outside. The pedal brake works on the transmission, and the handbrake on drums on the rear wheels.

A pressed-steel chassis of conventional type has semi-elliptic front springs, while the rear axle is located by two radius arms splayed rearward from the front universal joint on the shaft final drive and suspended by three-quarter-elliptic leaf springs. The wheelbase measures 130 inches, the front track is 51.8 inches, and the rear track slightly wider at 52 inches. This Adler has wooden artillery wheels, but Rudge-Whitworth wire type were optional; 815x105-mm tires are fitted.

Adler cars were imported into England in considerable numbers before World War I by the coach-building concern of Morgan and Co. of Leighton Buzzard; the model to be seen at Turin has a fine example of the bodywork, with two semi-open seats at the front and a fully enclosed rear compartment. The upholstery is in velvet, the roof can be partially opened, and there is a speaking tube for communication with the driver. The actual finish of the body panels and other surfaces is superb.

This car just preceded the era of electric lighting and mechanical starting. Thus it is equipped with a pair of imposing acetylene headlamps, fed by a centralized gas generator, and two oil sidelamps. There is a luggage rack on the roof; a spare wheel carrying a nonperiod tire is mounted on the offside runningboard by the driver's door. Comfort and reliability were the prior objectives in this car, and its maximum speed was only 37 mph.

The Adler before the gates of the Stupinigi Palace near Turin (left) and (below) the speaking tube for giving the driver his instructions, an indispensable accessory for the chauffeur-driven car of the day.

Aquila Italia 25/30

1912

The Aquila Italiana make of car was founded in Turin in 1906. Its designer was Giulio Cesare Cappa, one of the best automobile engineers and inventors in Italy. His car, which was manufactured both in four- and six-cylinder forms, enjoyed a period of considerable success in competitions before World War I, in the hands of racing drivers like Marsaglia, Beria d'Argentina, and Costantini.

The model illustrated here, which can be seen at the Biscaretti museum, is the six-cylinder racing car of 1912. Its engine carries Cappa's technical stamp, having a very compact monobloc casting completely enclosed in order to protect the mechanical parts. The bore is 82 mm and the stroke 132 mm, giving a total displacement of 4,182 cc.

Although termed the 25/30 for fiscal reasons, its actual power output was 60 horsepower at 3,600 rpm. This crankshaft speed is very high for the time. It was realized by Cappa's bold use of ball-race main bearings, aluminum pistons, and tubular connecting rods, all of which considerably reduced the reciprocating weight.

The engine has overhead inlet valves and side exhaust valves, all operated by a single camshaft situated in the left-hand side of the crankcase. Water cooling is employed with pump and radiator, and there is pressure lubrication, high-tension magneto ignition, and a single carburetor of Aquila Italiana manufacture.

Transmission is through a multiple disk clutch and a four-speed gearbox, which is separate from the engine, but is carried in a single cast-aluminum cradle linked with the engine and housing the clutch. Final drive is by propeller shaft to a rigid rear axle, suspended on three-quarter elliptic leaf springs. Front suspension is by semi-elliptics, and an advanced feature is the use of an early form of hydraulic shock absorber to the front axle.

The chassis is of conventional type with pressed-steel side members. It is adapted from a normal production touring model and not specially designed for racing, when no doubt it would have been shorter. The wheelbase measures 120 inches and the tracks are 57 inches front and rear. Standard artillery wheels of Sankey steel type are used, and the tires are 820x120-mm front and rear. Braking is by large finned drums on the rear wheels, served by the handbrake, and a drum brake on the transmission, which is actuated by the pedal. Weight of the car is about 2,200 pounds, and the maximum speed close to 80 mph.

It looks rakish, but this racing Aquila Italiana is clearly based on a touring chassis. Note the hydraulic front shock absorbers, among the first used on a racing car. It could reach almost 80 mph.

Panhard et Levassor X17SS

1912

This very elegant example of a pre-World War I classic motor car by the famous French firm of Panhard et Levassor is a much admired exhibit at the Biscaretti museum. It is powered by a sleeve-valve engine, built by Panhard under Knight patents, wherein double sleeves are actuated by connecting rods from a camshaft, alternately covering and uncovering the inlet and exhaust ports. It was a silent, reliable form of valve gear, although it produced excessive oil smoke in the exhaust, which would bring disapproval in these days of anti-pollution measures.

The engine is a front-mounted, four-cylinder unit cast in two blocks. The dimensions are 80x130 mm, and it has a total capacity of 2,614 cc. The cylinder heads are completely flat and detachable for maintenance of the sleeves. A Panhard carburetor is fitted, and a high-tension magneto is driven off the camshaft, which also

suspension is by conventional semi-elliptic leaf springs, but the rear is unusual in having fully elliptic springs—that is, two semi-elliptics one above the other, the top one inverted. The rear axle is also equipped with friction shock absorbers to counteract bounce from spring reaction.

That striking bodywork with open driving seat is known as a Coupe de Ville. The saloon passenger compartment is specially heated by means of hot water from the engine circulating through piping. There is a speaking tube for communication with the driver and a handsome brass kilometer gauge recording trip and total distance covered.

The radiator cap (below) illustrates the fable of the hare and the tortoise above the rather curious motto for a motor car—"rien ne sert de courir" ("there's no point in hurrying"). The noiseless engine of this 2,750-pound car allowed it to reach a maximum speed of about 40 mph.

drives the water pump. Engine lubrication is by pressure, with the feed variable according to the position of the accelerator. The output is about 22 horsepower at 1,200 rpm, and such an engine will have been notably smooth in running.

The clutch is the single wet-plate type running in oil, and it transmits to a separate four-speed gearbox with its gearchange lever moving in a toothed gate. The propeller shaft final drive is enclosed in a torque tube with a spherical joint at the end of the gearbox. The casing of this gearbox and the rear axle housing are both made in aluminum. Braking with both hand and pedal operation, is through large-diameter drums on the rear wheels only. The wheels are wooden artillery type, fitted with 820x120-mm tires of questionable authenticity.

The Panhard's chassis is a strong affair with two pressed longitudinal members and cross-pieces. Front

Isotta Fraschini Type 8
1920

Isotta Fraschini cars in the 1920s were large, extremely elegant, and superbly finished, putting them in direct competition with Hispano-Suiza, Rolls-Royce, and the big American makes.

The Type 8 as seen at the Biscaretti museum is the impressive design with which the Milan-based company resumed car manufacture after World War I, in which they were busily occupied building aero and marine engines. The car has a massive in-line, eight-cylinder engine with vertical overhead valves operated by push-rods and short rocker arms; the timing gear is driven by chain.

Bore and stroke dimensions are 85x130 mm, giving a total displacement of 5,901 cc. With a compression ratio of 5:1, the power developed at 2,200 rpm was only 80 horsepower, which meant that this engine was largely unstressed and, therefore, very smooth-running and reliable. It has a one-piece cylinder block and combustion chambers in cast iron, with shallow paired heads.

The crankshaft of the Type 8 runs in nine massive main bearings. Other features include pressure lubrication, tubular connecting rods, twin Zenith carburetors and Bosch magneto ignition, together with a special easy starting device. The crankcase is of aluminum, and cooling is by centrifugal pump and fan.

A multiple disk clutch takes the drive to an integral three-speed gearbox, and a torque tube propeller shaft and spiral bevel final drive complete the transmission line. On such a large car the chassis is naturally a massive affair, but it is well proportioned and the side members are braced by the engine and four cross-pieces. The rigid axles are suspended front and rear by semi-elliptic leaf springs, while the rear axle also has two Houdaille hydraulic shock absorbers.

As is well known, designer Cattaneo had enthusiastically supported the fitting of front wheel brakes ever since 1910, and so the Type 8 has a complete mechanical braking system on all four wheels, operated through a mechanical-assist unit to reduce required pedal pressure, the handbrake working on the rear wheels.

The car is fitted with wire-spoked wheels carrying 895x135 mm tires. Some of the cars had Sankey steel artillery-type wheels as an option. The wheelbase is 145.5 inches, and the track measures 55.5 inches both front and rear. A characteristic feature of this Isotta Fraschini is the triple lever control to ensure perfect regulation of the engine in all running conditions; one lever works the ignition, the second the throttle, and the third the air/gas mixture. An adjustable steering column is yet another special feature of this very special car.

One of the largest Italian cars of all times, this Isotta Fraschini weighs 3,500 pounds, and carried its passengers in comfort at 78 mph.

Lancia Trikappa

1922

Vincenzo Lancia had planned to name all his cars after letters in the Greek alphabet, but when he got to Kappa he decided to stay with this letter for several models while working on the new and legendary car to be known as the Lambda. Thus, after the ordinary Kappa model and the Dikappa, which was, practically speaking, a sports version of the first, there appeared in 1922 the Trikappa.

This car was completely different from the first two in that the enginé, instead of having four cylinders, had eight of them, arranged in a narrow vee. This was not the first large-engined Lancia, for the firm had already built a 12-cylinder model, which did not go into production, but was certainly one of its biggest. Its resemblance to its brilliant successor, the Lambda, is apparent in the example at the Biscaretti museum.

The narrow V-8 engine has a bore and stroke of 75x130 mm, giving a total displacement of 4,594 cc. The cylinder block is a single casting, a notable engineering feat at that time, and overhead valves are operated by a single central overhead camshaft. This is driven by a vertical shaft from the crankshaft. A Zenith carburetor, high-tension magneto, pressure lubrication, and water cooling are other features, and the power output of this remarkable engine is 98 horsepower at 2,500 rpm.

A multiple dry-plate clutch takes the drive to a four-speed gearbox in unit with the engine, and then by drive shaft to the rear axle. Apart from the engine, the Trikappa was of classic conventional design, having a separate chassis with pressed-steel side members and cross-bracing, and semi-elliptic leaf spring suspension to both front and rear axles, assisted by friction shock absorbers all around.

Braking is mechanically operated on all four wheels, and Rudge-Whitworth type wire wheels with center lock fixing are fitted, mounting 895x135-mm tires. The wheelbase is 133 inches, and the tracks front and rear are 53 inches. Thanks to its exceptional power, the Trikappa had an excellent performance, with a maximum speed of 80 mph. Even though this model did not remain long in production, it proved the principle of the narrow angle vee engine, subsequently so successful in the Lambda.

Only 850 Lancia Trikappas were built, so they are extremely rare today. The car weighs about 2,850 pounds and could reach 80 mph.

Citroën C3

1923

The small Citroën built between 1922 and 1926 was known on the Continent as the 5CV, where they also called it the Citron, that is, the lemon, because that was its usual color. Its official factory designation was the model C, with the numbers 2 and 3 to indicate variations on the basic design. The example at the Biscaretti museum is a C3. It has a four-cylinder, in-line, monobloc engine with the cylinders and detachable head in cast iron, an aluminum crankcase, and a bore and stroke of 55x90 mm.

Total cylinder capacity is 855 cc, and the actual power produced was 11 horsepower (5 horsepower French fiscal rating) at a maximum of 2,600 rpm. This game little engine has a two-bearing crankshaft, water cooling with thermosiphon circulation, a Bendix coil ignition system, and electric starter.

A single dry-plate clutch transmits the drive to a conventional gearbox in unit with the engine; there are three speeds and reverse, and final drive is through a torque tube to the rear axle. Braking is by hand lever to the rear wheels and by pedal to the transmission.

The chassis of the C3 is a simple structure of channel section members, and the suspension is by quarter-elliptic leaf springs at front and rear. Pressed-steel disk wheels, which many thought were ugly at the time, were essentially practical and cheaper to manufacture.

The wheelbase is 92.5 inches, and the track 46.5 inches at front and rear. An overall length of only 128 inches and width of 53 inches made the 5CV extremely handy for maneuvering into tight spaces. With this asset, plus those of cheapness, economical running, and an apparent indestructability, these little two-seater Citroëns sold in many thousands. Large numbers came to Britain, where they were known as Cloverleafs by reason of their open "torpedo" body with upturned tail. A curious feature, obviously to keep manufacturing costs down, was that the body had only one door, situated on the passenger's side, while on the driver's side the spare wheel was firmly bolted to the runningboard.

With a weight of only 1,300 pounds (590 kg), the 11-horsepower engine could work the car up to a speed of about 38 mph, but this took time. The braking was not a strong point either. Yet the Citron remained one of the "character" cars on the roads of the 1920s.

The little Citroën with its characteristic pointed tail was usually painted yellow and was quickly nicknamed "citron," or lemon. As light as it is small (1,300 pounds), this very popular car could reach 38 mph.

Maserati Type 26B

1928

This is the kind of car in which Alfieri Maserati established the trident make in racing before it began to win International Grands Prix.

The Maserati brothers founded their modest racing car factory at Bologna in 1926, with the creation of an eight-cylinder model called the Type 26. This had a cylinder capacity of 1,500 cc and was driven by Alfieri Maserati, one of the founders of the firm, to several successes in Italian events. In order to meet ever-increasing demands for more power and speed, the car was improved and fitted with a larger engine of 2 liters, when it became known as the 26B.

A rare surviving example of this car can be seen at the Biscaretti museum. It is a typical racing car of the time, with a low, offset two-seater body and front-mounted, in-line, eight-cylinder engine. The dimensions are 62 mm bore and 82 mm stroke, giving it a total displacement of 1,980 cc. With a single Roots-type supercharger and a compression ratio of 5.6:1, this engine produced 155

horsepower at 5,300 rpm, giving the car a speed of about 112 mph.

Both the cylinder block and the head are in cast iron, with the overhead valves each disposed at an angle of 45 degrees. Twin gear-driven overhead camshafts actuate the valves, the engine is water cooled and pressure lubricated, and ignition is by high-tension magneto.

The engine is in unit with a multiple-disk dry-plate clutch and four-speed gearbox, and final drive is by propeller shaft passing down the center of the chassis, with the driver's seat to the right of it. The chassis is of conventional type, with pressed-steel side members having a dropped center section to lower the car, with tubular cross-bracing. A rigid front axle is suspended by semi-elliptic leaf springs, and these are also employed at the rear, with friction-type shock absorbers fitted all around.

The Maserati has large-diameter, mechanically operated drum brakes to all four wheels, which are of Rudge-Whitworth wire type with quick-release hubs and "knock-off" caps to permit speedy tire changes during a long race. Tire size is 5.50x18 inches. The wheelbase is 104 inches, the track 53 inches, and the weight 1,590 pounds (720 kg).

As befits a racing car, the Maserati is well streamlined with steeply inclined radiator and a pointed tail, in which the fuel tank is housed. This carries some 21 gallons; the fuel is basically gas with a small proportion of benzole plus oil to lubricate the supercharger.

Trossi Monaco

1935

Among the many racing cars that stand out from the ordinary, the Trossi-Monaco Grand Prix car of 1935 is certainly one of the most remarkable for its theoretical solutions to the problems of obtaining high performance. It was designed and built by the engineer Augusto Monaco with the financial help of the racing driver Count Carlo-Felice Trossi.

The most extraordinary part of the car is the engine. This is an air-cooled, two-stroke radial, apparently with eight cylinders but in fact with sixteen, arranged in two rows in such a way that each pair of cylinders, front and rear, share a common cylinder head and combustion chamber. The rear cylinders contain the inlet ports and the front cylinders contain the exhaust ports; mixture from twin Zenith carburetors is forced in by twin Roots-type superchargers and ignited by twin magnetos and one spark plug to each pair of cylinders.

The crankshaft runs in roller bearings and has a "master" connecting rod that carries seven other articulated rods, each forked to carry two pistons. The cylinders measure 65x75-mm bore and stroke, and total cylinder capacity is 3,982 cc. The theoretical power output was 250 horsepower at 6,000 rpm, but Monaco encountered many overheating and other troubles with this engine.

Resembling a radial-engined aircraft of the 1930s era, the Trossi carried its engine well forward on the nose, and the rest of the car resembled an aircraft fuselage. Indeed, it was constructed in similar fashion, having a frame of welded tubes with light alloy panels.

The surprises do not end there, for the 1,550-pound car has front-wheel drive; power from the engine is transmitted back through a multi-plate clutch to a four-speed gearbox, then forward again to the front wheels via a differential and double universal-jointed half-shafts.

Other interesting features include independent suspension to all four wheels by means of wishbones, bell-cranks and horizontal coil springs, and hydraulic brakes all around. Designed for speed well in excess of 130 mph, the Trossi, alas, was too complicated to succeed, and never actually raced.

This single photograph of an exceptional car emphasizes the concentrated power of the 16-cylinder, two-stroke radial engine.

Cisitalia 202

1948

This beautiful little Cisitalia coupe, with its low, flowing lines by the great coachbuilder Pininfarina, is one of the first on which the wings are no longer separate but merge into the body. It is a car that set the style for an entire epoch, while mechanically, too, this clever Turin design established new ways of creating a light, maneuverable sports car out of ordinary quantity production components.

The engine of the Cisitalia 202 is, in fact, derived from the standard overhead valve FIAT 1100, having the same dimensions of 68x75-mm bore and stroke and a capacity of 1,089 cc. So far as precision and tuning is concerned, however, it is in a different class. The crankshaft is counter-balanced, while special connecting rods and pistons and larger valves are fitted. With a compression ratio of 7.5:1 plus modified ports and manifolding, this engine could comfortably produce 50 horsepower at 5,500 rpm, giving the car lively acceleration and a maximum speed above 95 mph.

The specification includes a single vertical carburetor, coil and distributor ignition, water cooling with pump and radiator, and pressure lubrication with an oil cooler combined with the water radiator. The cylinder block is of cast iron, and the head of light alloy; there were higher-tuned multi-carburetor variants available.

A single dry-plate clutch takes the drive to a four-speed gearbox in unit with the engine, and then through a propeller shaft to a rigid rear axle with hypoid bevel final drive.

The Cisitalia's chassis is an advanced structure of welded tubes known as a "space frame," and it is both lighter and stronger than a conventional frame, which has stout side members to give beam strength. Front suspension is independent by means of wishbones and a transverse leaf spring, while the non-independent rear springing is by coils. There are hydraulic shock absorbers at front and rear.

Wire wheels with light alloy rims are fitted with 5x15-inch tires, and the drum brakes are hydraulically oper-

ated. The wheelbase is 94.5 inches and the tracks 49 inches front and rear. Pininfarina built the low, aerodynamic coupe body in light alloy; faster variations in spider and ultra-light coupe forms were also built for competition purposes. In fact, a factory-prepared spider model finished second in the 1947 Mille Miglia.

Many years have passed since the Cisitalia was manufactured, but the pure lines of this car still inspire designers of modern cars. It is outstanding for its lack of complexity or superfluous ornamentation and the decisiveness of its lines. It weighed just over 1,940 pounds and had a maximum speed of 97 mph.

$\mathscr{FIAT}$ $\mathscr{Turbine\ Car}$

1954

In 1954 the FIAT Company produced an experimental car that was powered by a gas turbine engine. Such a project had been studied for years, and the car was constructed to provide a practical evaluation of this new type of power unit and its potential in a car. The resultant vehicle, which can be seen on display at the Biscaretti museum, comes halfway between an ordinary automobile and something out of science fiction. The outward appearance, though it is striking, does not depart very far from FIAT's normal sports models of the early 1950s, and indeed, the makers utilized many components from the production line, in particular the four-wheel independent suspension units from their 1952 8-V sporting model.

The most important element in this experimental car is, of course, the turbo-unit, which comprises a two-stage centrifugal compressor, a two-stage turbine, and a drive turbine, with three interlinked combustion chambers. A reduction gear brings down the shaft speed of the drive turbine from its 22,000-rpm maximum to around 4,000 rpm for transmitting the drive to the rear wheels.

This power unit is installed, in a special sound-damped compartment, ahead of the rear wheels and behind the two seats for driver and passenger. No gears are used, and the car is controlled only by the accelerator and the brakes. The air inlet for the compressors is in the nose, adorned with a chromed grille, and the exhaust for spent gases passes out of a large chromed vent in the tail.

No heat exchanger was fitted to the car, although its use was considered during development.

The frame of the FIAT *vettura sperimentale a turbina* is made up of longitudinal and transverse tubes, and the Type 8-V suspension units have double wishbones and coil springs at front and rear. There are hydraulically operated drum brakes on the four wheels, and these were hard-used during development runs since there is no retarding effect from a turbine when it is shut off, as with a normal internal combustion unit. Two fuel tanks are situated low down on either side of the power unit.

The wheelbase measures 94.5 inches and the tracks are 51 inches at both front and rear. Quick-release wire wheels with "knock-off" hubcaps, as used on the FIAT 8-V sports coupe, are fitted and carry 5.5x15-inch tires. The body shape was the subject of careful study during wind-tunnel research; it has a penetration coefficient equal to 0.14. The vertical rear fins were intended to guarantee high speed stability. Weight of the car is 2,200 pounds and maximum speed is a theoretical 155 mph.

A laboratory on four wheels is an appropriate definition of a car on which the dashboard resembles the control panel of a power station. Although built for experimental purposes only, much care was taken with the detail work and finish on the body of the turbine-powered FIAT, and thus it could be taken for an elegant custom-built dream car.

MUSEO NAZIONALE DELLA SCIENZA E DELLA TECNICA LEONARDO DA VINCI

adapted first as a hospital and then as a barracks, which resulted in various alterations that spoiled its original appearance.

Only after the Second World War was the old building adapted as a museum under the keen direction of Ucelli, who was able from a heap of ruins to restore its original appearance and to make the interior suitable for exhibition purposes. The museum was inaugurated in 1953 and is, therefore, one of the most recent from a historical point of view; yet the building itself and the various collections give an impression of imposing antiquity.

For the inauguration, an exhibition dedicated to Leonardo da Vinci was staged; it was a memorable exposition, perhaps unique in the world for the richness and variety of its displays. It began the active life of the museum and also gave it its name.

The original building has continually had new sections added to it; for example, a new railway section, which is part of the larger land transport section, and a big pavilion, which houses a complete sailing ship and a part of the Italian trans-Atlantic ship, the *Conte Biancamano.* The automobile section is approached through various oth-er displays, such as those on mineral research, basic mechanics, and early engines, which make an impressive panorama of man's technical accomplishments.

The actual car section is not very big, but it contains numerous "pieces" that in many cases are the only ones of their kind in existence and are, therefore, of great historical and technical value and interest.

To make the collection more complete, and to tell the story of land locomotion more fully, the full-sized vehicles are supplemented by scale models, which illustrate the most important achievements from Cugnot's famous three-wheeled tractor and de Rivaz's motorized cart to Bordino's steam *diligence,* and so on. And, of course, the visitor's interest need not end with the automobile exhibits, because there are other sections on sea and air transport, physics and various crafts—and all the worth a visit, even though it may be brief lastly, in rooms set aside for meetings and lectures—the *Sala Del Cenacolo* (the ancient refectory) and the *Sala dell Colonne* (once the monastery library) one becomes richly aware of the superb 16th-century monastic origins of the building.

Bianchi 8-hp

1901

The little Bianchi in the Leonardo da Vinci museum is one of the oldest Italian motor cars to have been preserved almost intact. The Bianchi Company was founded in 1885 as a firm of bicycle manufacturers and began building motor vehicles in 1899. Thus it is one of the oldest concerns in Italy and, indeed, in the world; yet it still operates today, albeit after a series of changes of ownership, as the present-day Autobianchi organization within the FIAT group.

The 8-horsepower model dated 1901 was a fairly well-perfected *vetturetta,* as light motor cars were then called in Italy. Edoardo Bianchi had had much experience with motor cars, but he didn't build his own engines at that time. The engine in his 8-horsepower model is a single-cylinder de Dion with a 100-mm bore and 120-mm stroke, and a cylinder capacity of 942.5 cc.

There is some doubt as to the year in which this car

Although externally similar to many other cars of the period, this early Italian open-tourer has some original features such as the rack-and-pinion steering. It is very small, with a wheelbase of only 60 inches and a weight of only 880 pounds, but thanks to its 8-horsepower single-cylinder de Dion engine, it managed a staunch 18 mph with two passengers.

really was built, but since its engine is of a type that de Dion seems not to have produced until 1902, one tends to believe those authorities who suggest that this Bianchi was built in 1903 and not 1901. The engine has water cooling—a pump driven off the rear end of the gearbox shaft circulating the water—an automatically operated inlet valve, and mechanically operated exhaust valve.

The engine is mounted in the front of the car (at a time when many still kept it at the rear) and drives through a three-speed gearbox with reverse—a real luxury for such a small car in those days—and then by shaft to the rear axle—again an advanced feature when so many used chains. The hood is the alligator type, as pioneered by Renault, and indeed much of this Bianchi design, apart from the primitive forward-mounted tubular radia-

tor on the Italian product, would seem to have been inspired by the Renault tourer.

Interesting features of the car include an early form of rack-and-pinion steering and the neat grouping of the control levers on the steering column. With ready access to steel tubing for their bicycles, it is not surprising that this Bianchi has a frame made up of steel tubes. The suspension both at front and rear is fully elliptic, and the rear axle is located longitudinally by two radius arms.

Braking is by external-contracting bands on the rear wheels, which are of wire-spoked type, carrying 26x3-inch pneumatic tires. The wheelbase is 60 inches, and the front and rear tracks are 40 inches and 42 inches respectively. With its open two-seater bodywork of elegant "horseless carriage" form, including the buttoned and pleated leather seats, this car weighed about 880 pounds and must have been light and easy to handle. Thanks to its robust 8-horsepower de Dion engine, moreover, the little Bianchi could easily reach 18 mph—an ideal early shopping vehicle!

Designed to take the place of the highly successful Type 158 Alfetta, this flat-12 rear-engined car brings to mind in many ways the Grand Prix Cisitalia subsequently designed by Porsche and, like it, never advanced beyond the experimental stage, serving only to adorn a museum.

Alfa Romeo 512

1939

Just before the outbreak of war in 1939, the Alfa Romeo technicians began work on a new rear-engined racing car for the 1,500-cc class; this car was to surpass and supersede the well-known Type 158 Alfetta, built for Alfa by Enzo Ferrari. In fact, it is said that this new design, the work of the Spanish engineer Wilfredo Ricart, was one of the causes of the break between Ferrari and the Milanese company.

Be that as it may, the car labeled the 512 was built in 1940, improved in 1941, and then laid up for the rest of the war. When peace came again, however, the urgent need to restart production of road cars persuaded the company to abandon the 512 and rely on the more conventional Alfetta racers, which certainly proved their capability by dominating the scene for several more years. Moreover, it is said that the rear-engined car was difficult to handle because of the driver's position, which was too far forward, and poor weight distribution.

Whatever the pros and cons of the design, it is very interesting to be able to study the actual car, now preserved at the Leonardo da Vinci museum. The engine is a flat-12 in two horizontally opposed banks of six cylinders, located behind the driver and ahead of the rear wheels, forming a combined unit with the gearbox and final drive. Cylinder dimensions are 54-mm bore and 54.2-mm stroke, giving an overall displacement of 1,490 cc.

The power achieved on the test bench was very high for the time, being 335 horsepower at 8,600 rpm, with more promised after further development. Two superchargers and a three-barrel Weber carburetor fed this thirsty engine its methanol-based fuel diet at a pressure of 32 pounds per square inch. There are gear-driven twin overhead camshafts to each bank of cylinders, and the detachable heads and blocks are cast in light alloy. Hairpin-type valve springs are employed, and ignition is by twin Bosch magnetos, one to each bank. Copious pressure lubrication and water cooling from the front-mounted radiator are other features of the design.

A dry multiple-disk clutch transmits the drive to a five-speed gearbox behind the rear axle, and a German ZF-type limited-slip differential is fitted. Front suspen-

sion is independent by double wishbones and longitudinal torsion bars, and at the rear a de Dion type axle is employed, with the beam ahead of the axle line and large radius arms running to the rear, converging on a central trunnion. The wheelbase of the 512 is approximately 96 inches and the tracks 52 inches front and rear. Hydraulically operated drum brakes are featured all around, and the Rudge-type quickly detachable wire wheels carry 7x18-inch tires at the rear and 5.25x17-inch at the front. Even with the weight of 60 gallons of fuel on board, maximum speed of this car, which never raced, is an estimated 190 mph.

Nardi 750-cc

1955

The story of this strange car is somewhat obscure, and since its constructor, Enrico Nardi, is no longer alive, we can only deduce the facts from other sources. The car was apparently commissioned by a sportsman from north of the Alps, a certain Monsieur Damonte, who was to drive it in the Le Mans 24-Hour Race in 1955, together with his friend Crovetto. The two Frenchmen were responsible for its unusual layout, which is based on the "bisiluro" or "twin-fuselage" type of car built for record-breaking attempts, notably by the Italian Piero Taruffi.

In the case of the Nardi, however, the two fuselages, one of which contains the engine and transmission, and the other the driver, are joined together by a slender central section, which contains the radiator and a "seat." The engine is housed in the left boom, or fuselage, and is

an in-line, four-cylinder unit built by Giannini. The bore and stroke are 63x59 mm, and the total capacity 747 cc, the car competing in the 750-cc category at Le Mans.

This little engine has twin overhead camshafts and four single carburetors; the power output is 64 horsepower at 7,200 rpm, which compares well with the ordinary sports version of the Giannini unit, giving only 47 horsepower. A single dry-plate clutch takes the drive to a four-speed gearbox, and then by an angled drive shaft to the differential/final drive unit on the inside of the near-side rear wheel. Thus the entire engine and transmission are contained in the nearside boom.

The chassis is a shallow tubular structure, with independent front suspension of Lancia Ardea type; that is, vertical pillars containing coil springs. A rigid, "live" rear axle is used, with semi-elliptic leaf springing, and, as can be seen, all components are admirably contained within the very well-streamlined bodywork. Le Mans regulations required a second seat for a theoretical passenger, so the Nardi 750 was provided with a very shallow compartment in the center next to the driver. They rendered it still more farcical as a "sports car" by utilizing its lid as an air brake! The surface radiator is beautifully merged into the bodywork, and the 15-inch wheels are completely covered in. The car performed disappointingly at Le Mans, retiring early, and although also intended for record breaking, the Nardi never reappeared in competition.

A radically different racing and record car, the Nardi's surface-type radiator follows the contours of the body. The hatch in the center section opened up to act as a windbrake. Over 108 mph was claimed for this beautifully streamlined, 880-pound car, but it was never fully developed, retired early at Le Mans in 1955, and broke no records.

MUSEO STORICO ALFA ROMEO

Realizing the ever-mounting importance attached nowadays to the history of the automobile, Alfa Romeo decided to create a museum and thus maintain a "living" record of its many fine products built through the years.

While awaiting a final, definitive home, a considerable number of cars have been collected, restored, and preserved in a section of the new Alfa Romeo factory at Arese. At present this collection contains some thirty cars, illustrating the very full history of the firm, which began in 1910 as the heir to a branch of the French Darracq Company. Since then the make has pursued a vigorous sporting policy, with racing serving as the test-bed for better design, and has produced many fine cars that became legendary in their own time and are now "classics."

Fortunately, many examples of these have been preserved, among them the glorious P2 and P3 (or Type B) Grand Prix racing cars, the six-cylinder 1750 sports, which is perhaps the most famous car ever produced by Alfa Romeo, and the legendary Type 158 Formula 1 car with which Farina and Fangio won the World Championship titles in 1950 and 1951 respectively. There are numerous other cars too, some of them normal production models, but all with that strong sporting characteristic which is the very hallmark of Alfa Romeo.

The curator of this museum is Luigi Fusi, a tremendous car enthusiast who has been employed by the company ever since 1920, working on the design of many cars, both racing and touring models. Fusi is also the author of an absorbing book containing data, drawings, and photographs of all the cars built by Alfa Romeo from 1910 until 1965.

The museum at Arese is a living thing, with a continually increasing number of cars on display, and is visited by an ever-growing public. Currently the precious cars are housed in a big room of one of the buildings in the factory complex, but this is a temporary arrangement. Eventually more permanent accommodation will be found, and the collection can then be shown to the public to better advantage.

It is also certain that the collection will gradually be enlarged, both by the discovery of "new" examples of historic importance and by the addition of new models that will be landmarks in automobile development. One such example is the special Carabo, constructed by the famous coachbuilder Bertone on an Alfa Romeo V-8-engined Type 33 chassis. Taking the form of an ultra-low two-seater coupe of the future, this car was the sensation of the 1968 Paris Salon when first shown. Later it was sold to a client, but Alfa Romeo managed to stop the sale and reserve it for the museum.

Alfa 24-hp

1910

As is well known, Alfa Romeo sprang from an Italian branch of the French Darracq Company. This project was unsuccessful, and in 1909 Darracq Italiana was reconstructed with all-Italian capital and became the Societa Anonima Lombarda Fabbrica Automobili (The Lombardy Car Manufacturing Company) or, using the initials only, ALFA. The name Romeo was not added until after World War I, when engineer Nicola Romeo took over the firm.

In the autumn of 1909, therefore, the new Alfa company laid plans for a completely fresh car to replace the Darracq pattern. Designed by Giuseppe Merosi, the first 24-horsepower model is a fairly classical, conventional type; yet it already showed signs of the path the company was to follow to high-performance touring cars.

Its in-line, four-cylinder engine has a cast-iron monobloc with fixed head, and there are side-by-side valves, operated by a camshaft housed in the crankcase. This is cast in aluminum and has three bearings for the crankshaft and four attachment lugs for fixing to the chassis. Bore and stroke are 100x130 mm, giving a cylinder capacity of 4,084 cc. Power output is 42 horsepower at 2,200 rpm, later raised to 49 horsepower at 2,400 rpm in the long career of this very sturdy model.

The specification also includes a vertical carburetor,

This early production model Alfa had no pretensions toward sporting appearance, but its lively performance and over 60 mph maximum helped put it on the road to speed competitions.

magneto ignition, pressure lubrication, and water cooling with pump and fan. The transmission consists of a dry multiple-disk clutch and a separate gearbox with four speeds and reverse, with final drive by torque tube to the live rear axle.

The chassis of the Alfa 24-horsepower is made up of longitudinal members and C-shaped pressed-steel cross members; the suspension is by semi-elliptic leaf springs at front and rear, without the assistance of shock absorbers. Drum-type brakes, operated by hand and pedal, are fitted to the rear wheels only. The wooden-spoked wheels are fitted with 820x120-mm tires.

With a 126-inch wheelbase and 53-inch front and rear tracks, this is quite a spacious car. The open torpedo version at the da Vinci Museum could seat six or seven. It weighed 2,200 pounds and its speed of over 62 mph was exceptional. A racing version of the 24-horsepower Alfa, with two seats and spare wheels strapped to the frame, was unlucky not to win its first race, the 1911 Targa Florio; the driver was blinded by mud after leading two of the three long rounds.

Alfa Romeo RL Super Sport

1925

Several versions of this car were built by Alfa Romeo during the 1920s—the 1A and 2A series in 1922–23, the 3A and 4A in 1923–24, the 5A and 6A in 1925, and the 7A series in 1926–27. The RL typifies the Italian sporting car of the period with its vee radiator and windshield, flared fenders and wire wheels.

The engine is a six-cylinder overhead valve unit with bore and stroke of 76x110 mm and a cylinder capacity of 2,994 cc. The block is a single casting in iron, with a detachable head. in which the valves are operated by push rods and rocker arms. The crankshaft runs in four bearings, and the engine has twin vertical carburetors, high-tension magneto ignition, water cooling by pump and fan, and forced lubrication. Power output is 56 horsepower at 3,200 rpm.

Engine, clutch, and gearbox are in one unit, the clutch being of dry multiple-disk type and the gearbox having four forward speeds and reverse. The propeller shaft has two universal joints, and the rear axle housing is fabricated in sheet metal instead of the more usual casting. There is a transmission brake behind the gearbox connected to the handbrake and pedal-operated drum brakes on all four wheels.

The chassis is of classic type, with pressed-steel side members and riveted cross-bracing; the suspension is by semi-elliptic leaf springs all around, supplemented by friction shock absorbers. The 20-gallon gas tank is mounted at the rear. The RL Super Sport at the Alfa Romeo museum is distinguished by its special aluminum body finish, which is "engine turned" and then highly polished.

Dimensions of the car include a 124-inch wheelbase, 57-inch front and rear tracks, and a weight of 3,850 pounds. Rudge-Whitworth-type wire wheels with splined quick-release hubs and knock-off caps are fitted, and the tires are 120x820 mm all around. It is quite a heavy car for an open four/five seater, which makes its maximum speed of over 80 mph all the more creditable.

Shorter wheelbase racing versions of the Alfa Romeo RL were prepared by the factory and raced with success, one winning the Targa Florio outright in 1923.

The vee-shaped radiator and double badges appeared only on this Alfa Romeo model, the vee motif being continued in the divided windshield. Note the distinctive polished metal bodywork on this rare example of the six-cylinder, pushrod, overhead valve car.

Alfa Romeo 6C 1750 SS

1929

Produced from 1929 until 1932, the Alfa Romeo Type 6C 1750 model was certainly one of the most famous ever built by the Milanese firm. It was a direct development of the preceding model, the 6C 1500, most of whose characteristics it kept, such as the structure of the engine and the weight. Thanks to its increased cylinder capacity, however, the 1750 had appreciably greater torque and higher performance.

The first car was revealed at the 1929 Rome Motor Show in January, and it made its racing debut three months later in the Mille Miglia—and promptly won this extremely grueling 1,000-mile race across Italy. The model was produced in several versions—Touring, Sport, Super Sport, and Grand Sport; the example on display at Arese is a Super Sport or SS.

The basic makeup of the car is fairly orthodox; it is in the execution of the design and its performance that the Alfa Romeo 6C is outstanding. The frame is made up of two pressed-steel longitudinal members and crosspieces, while the front and rear suspension is by semi-elliptic leaf springs and friction shock absorbers; all these items are conventional, but they are exquisitely made and finely balanced.

The engine is a superb in-line, six-cylinder unit with twin overhead camshafts, and a 65x88-mm bore and stroke, giving a cylinder capacity of 1,752 cc and an output of 85 horsepower at 4,500 rpm. A supercharger is driven off the front end of the crankshaft, which runs in five bearings. The lower part of the engine is made in light alloy, but the head and block are in cast iron. The valves are angled at 45 degrees and the two camshafts are driven by a vertical shaft. Ignition is by battery, distributor, and coil, and pressure lubrication and water cooling are normal features.

Transmission on the 1750 is by dry multiple-disk clutch to a four-speed gearbox in unit with the engine. Drive to the rear axle is by torque tube, with a single universal joint behind the gearbox. The fuel tank is in the tail. Rudge-Whitworth quick-release wire wheels are fitted, and the tires are 27x4.75 in front and rear. The wheelbase is 108 inches and the track at front and rear measures 54 inches. Large-diameter drum brakes of great efficiency are fitted to all four wheels.

This lithe and agile machine could attain 90 mph, and with its clean, stark lines and swept fenders, it epitomizes the classic pre-war Alfa Romeo sports car.

Recalling old glories of Alfa Romeo's racing days, the six-cylinder 1750 Super Sport with Zagato two-seater "spider" body was one of the great sports cars of the late 1920s. Note the characteristic triple headlamps protected by a wire grille. This supercharged version could achieve 90 mph, with exceptional roadholding.

Alfa Romeo Type B

1932

This is one of the most famous and successful racing cars in motoring history. As the first single-seater to be built for Grand Prix racing, it was called the *monoposto* (single-seat), but its factory designation was the Type B. However, as the successor to the illustrious Alfa Romeo P2 racing car of the 1920s, it was also referred to unofficially as the P3. It was designed by Vittorio Jano. The Type B made its racing debut in the 1932 Italian Grand Prix, which it won, and it was driven to dozens of victories before becoming obsolete.

It has an eight-cylinder, in-line engine made in two blocks of four, divided by the central enclosed gear train that drives the twin overhead camshafts and twin superchargers. The bore is 65 mm and the stroke 100 mm, giving a total capacity of 2,654 cc. Block and head are a single casting in light alloy, with steel cylinder liners inserted. There are two valves per cylinder, angled to give 104 degrees between them, and they are operated by double overhead camshafts. The two superchargers are mounted, one on each side of the central gear drive, each feeding four cylinders at a pressure of 10 pounds per square inch. The maximum power produced is 215 horsepower at 5,600 rpm.

The gearbox has four forward speeds and reverse, and is in unit with the engine, while the clutch is of twin-plate disk type. The most interesting feature of the P3 Monoposto is undoubtedly the transmission. This has twin drive shafts that drive the rear axle through two separate sets of bevels, one each side of the axle, while the differential is in a housing just behind the gearbox, which also contains the gears that define the final drive. The object of this was to reduce the unsprung weight and to lower the central driver's seat.

Suspension is by semi-elliptic leaf springs all around, assisted by friction shock absorbers. The wheelbase is 104 inches (lengthened slightly in 1934), and the tracks are 53 inches at front and rear. Mechanically operated brakes are in very large-finned alloy drums on all four wheels, and the wheels themselves are Rudge-type wire spoked with quick-release hubs and carry 28x5.50 tires front and rear. In 1932 form this car had a weight of 1,540 pounds unladen and a speed of 144 mph.

This Type B Monoposto, or P3 as it is often called, is as pristine as when it came out of the factory.

Alfa Romeo Type 159
1951

The Type 159 is the final version of the renowned 1,500 cc straight-Eight supercharged *Alfetta,* the last single-seater racing car built by Alfa Romeo. At the beginning of its brilliant 13-year career, the car was designated the Type 158, denoting its engine's 1.5 liters and eight cylinders, and only in the last version, which came out in 1951, was it called the 159 to differentiate the improved car from previous ones.

This superb-looking racing car won its very first race—the Ciano Cup at Leghorn—in 1938, and its very last—the Spanish Grand Prix at Barcelona—in 1951, the victory that clinched that year's World Driver's Championship for Juan-Manuel Fangio. In between these years the Alfetta scored win after win, totaling over thirty, and establishing it as one of the world's really great racing cars.

Its engine, like that of the earlier P3 Monoposto, is a twin-supercharged, twin overhead camshaft straight-Eight, but there the similarity ends. The Type 159, which is so impressive an exhibit at the Arese Museum, has a 58x70-mm bore and stroke and a cylinder capacity of 1,479 cc. In 1938 it produced 195 horsepower at 7,200 rpm, but this was successively raised to 225, 254, 310, 350, 404, and 425 horsepower at 9,300 rpm in the 159 version, more than doubling the output!

To achieve this, the original single-stage supercharging was replaced by a two-stage system, while many other detail engine changes were made. The power is transmitted through a dry multiple-disk clutch and a universally jointed propeller shaft to a four-speed gearbox built in unit with the final drive on the rear axle. A limited-slip differential is fitted.

The chassis of the Type 159 is of "ladder" type, made with oval steel tube longitudinal supports and tubular crosspieces. Front suspension is by trailing links and by a transverse leaf spring, while at the rear is a de Dion-type axle, also employing a transverse leaf spring positioned behind the final drive housing. Telescopic hydraulic shock absorbers are fitted all around.

Huge drum brakes, pierced for ventilation, are hydraulically operated. The Rudge-type racing wheels are fitted with 7x18-inch tires at the rear and 5.50x17-inch

The classic beauty of the Alfetta in its final form is brought home by the photograph above. It represents the crowning point of the supercharged engine with a specific power of almost 300 horsepower per liter. It weighed under 1,550 pounds dry and could attain 186 mph.

at the front. The fuel consumption on this car was extremely high, and besides the large tail tank, there are two others along the body sides with a total capacity of 60 gallons. Its wheelbase is 97 inches and maximum speed around 186 mph.

MUSÉE DU CHÂTEAU DE GRANDSON

On the road from Lausanne to Neuchâtel, in a small village mirrored in the Lake of Neuchâtel itself, stands the Château de Grandson, home of the Grandson museum. At first sight, the Château scarcely looks real, so close is it to the popular conception of a fairy-tale castle, with its five towers and their dunce's cap roofs, the lofty embattled walls and massive wooden gates.

But everything is authentic in what has been called the loveliest castle in Switzerland, and one of the finest in Europe. It was almost in ruins when it was "discovered" by Georges Filipinetti, diplomat, businessman, lover of fine cars, and one whose name is very well known in recent years for his motor racing stable.

Now the Château de Grandson has been restored to its former splendor and houses a fabulous collection of medieval military equipment, weapons, armor, and a series of models of famous battles. Everything has been put into working order again, includ-

LAUSANNE

ing the torture chamber and the dungeons.

A small part of the castle is used as a private residence, but all the rest is open to the public. Monsieur Filipinetti's collection of cars is displayed in such a manner that it does not disturb the historical unity of the castle. The cars are, in fact, arranged in that part of the castle overlooking the rampart on the lakeside, which was once partly the barracks and partly a reception hall for guests to the castle.

The rough stone walls, several feet thick, are a fine background to the score of old cars conserved here. For the more recent sports cars there is a special room near the entrance lodge, on the walled side of the park. In all there are some thirty to forty vehicles, of which perhaps ten are kept in reserve so that they may be alternated with others on show.

Without doubt, quality makes up for the lack of quantity at the Grandson museum, many of the cars being unique, or extreme-ly rare, such as the Swiss Egg of 1895, which is the only one in existence and has the first known application of an automatic gearbox with an infinitely variable choice of ratios. Other rare Swiss makes are also to be seen, together with other interesting foreign touring, sporting, and racing cars.

Apart from the purely motoring and historical interest of the museum and castle, there is an intriguing episode regarding the branch of the Grandson family that settled in England in the 14th century. Catherine, one of the young ladies of the family, added her piece to history when she lost one of her garters—and it was the king himself, Edward III, who knelt to pick it up. After this incident, the king established the Order of the Garter, and young Catherine of Grandson passed into history under the name of Countess of Salisbury.

This lovely castle, poised between legend and reality, is particularly well worth visiting in spring and summer.

Egg
1895

This car, which was built by Rudolf Egg, a Zurich designer, is reputed to be the oldest surviving automobile built in Switzerland. It certainly dates back to before Egg's association with the Egli Company, which began in 1896, when the make became Egg and Egli.

The 1895 Egg has a Benz single-cylinder horizontal engine mounted at the rear, with a 130x150-mm bore and stroke, giving an engine capacity of 1,991 cc and 3 horsepower at 470 rpm. An evaporation carburetor is employed, ignition is by hot tube, and the engine has drip-feed lubrication. The cooling system works by water evaporation, with a scroll-shaped front condenser mounted below the radiator.

Of particular interest is the transmission, which is of the infinitely variable type (a later version of the same system can be seen on the 1902 Weber at the Grandson museum). In this antecedent of the modern DAF Variomatic transmission, there are two conical pulleys with respective diameters that can be varied reciprocally, the diameter of one increasing when the other is reduced. In addition, a lever allows the two pulleys to be extended simultaneously, so that the belt slackens and a clutch effect is obtained. Each of the two pulleys has a disk with several slots, which engages a conical retainer or cage.

The differential consists of cylindrical pinions instead of bevels and is completely exposed. Band brakes operate on the rear wheels, which are the wire-spoked type, carrying 3.00x26 tires on the front and 3.5x30 at the rear. The control lever for belt tension is located on the steering column, and a mechanical detail to be found today on cars with automatic transmission is a system of locking the rear wheels by means of a tooth or sprag engaging with the differential crown wheel.

The chassis of the Egg automobile is made of steel tubes, with a kind of sub-frame supporting the axles, suspended by leaf springs from the main chassis. The open four-seat bodywork is of the "vis-à-vis" (face-to-face) type, with the driver occupying the offside rear seat and using a two-handled tiller like a pair of handlebars as he motored along at the modest top speed of 11 mph (18 kph).

Details of the Egg's remarkable transmission can be seen on the left. The diameter of the drive pulleys can be varied by a form of bevel cage moving from right to left to expand the pulley. A final drive with spur gears is used. Believed to be the oldest surviving Swiss car, this 1895 Egg has a 2-liter single-cylinder, 3-horsepower Benz engine.

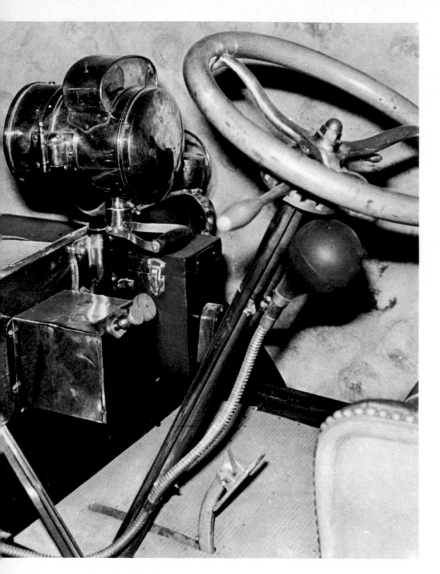

Cameron was one of many small American makes that had an
ephemeral existence in the early part of the century. One suspects that
the somewhat inadequate cooling system may have given Cameron
owners trouble! This car had shaft drive and gearbox on the rear axle.

Cameron 9-hp

1904

There can be few makes of car from any country that
have changed their addresses as often as did the Amer-
ican-built Cameron. Indeed, in its fairly brief existence
from when it was founded in 1902 to its final winding up
in 1919, there were no less than eight different com-
panies formed, each descending from the previous one,
and occupying six different places of manufacture!

Details of the various models built by Cameron are
hard to come by, and it is, therefore, interesting and
unexpected to find a well-restored example of the make
in the Grandson museum in Switzerland. The two-seater
to be seen there is a roadster, or what used to be called a
"runabout." The given date of manufacture, 1904, may
be questioned since in that year all Camerons were
apparently fitted with single-cylinder engines, whereas
this example has a two-cylinder unit thought not to have
been used before 1905.

Whatever the case may be, it is an interesting engine. It
has a side-valve, in-line vertical twin with air-cooling by
means of an open grille and a fan. Both inlet and exhaust
valves are mechanically operated, and the high-tension
ignition is of the trembler coil type.

A modern feature of this light, lively car is its shaft
drive from the engine and clutch to a two-speed gearbox
mounted on the rear axle, and incorporating the differential. It is also interesting to note that all the controls
for the driver, that is, accelerator, advance-and-retard,
and gear-change, are mounted on the steering column,
while the only lever is the handbrake, which acts on the
rear wheels. The steering wheel is on the left. A pump on
the dashboard works the engine lubrication by pressure.

The car at Grandson departs from catalog specification in having wire-spoked wheels instead of hickory
artillery-type, which were listed as standard. The tires
are 3.00x21. The chassis appears to be of wood, with
steel reinforcing plates and suspension supports attached
at the front. The suspension is by small semi-elliptic leaf
springs at the front, but by fully elliptic at the rear. The
car has a 73-inch wheelbase, and could attain a maximum speed of 22 mph (35 kph).

The Clément-Bayard make, which lived for 19 years from 1903 to 1922, had a fine reputation and enjoyed a huge market in its heyday. When the model now on display at Grandson was introduced, the manufacturer's catalog listed no less than 15 different models.

This sporty-looking two-seater was one of the smallest versions, and its design bears more than a passing resemblance to the rival Renault of the same period. The dashboard radiator and "coal scuttle" hood were features successfully employed by Renault, while the twin-cylinder engine is clearly Renault-inspired. Its cylinders are in line, and the dimensions are 75x120-mm bore and stroke, giving a displacement of 1,060 cc.

The car in the museum was a new model in 1909, for until that year the twin-cylinder engines had an 85x110-mm bore and stroke and a 1,248-cc capacity; the change was probably made so that the Twins and

Clement-Bayard
8-hp
1909

204

Fours should share the same bore and stroke, thereby easing production problems. The car has high-tension magneto ignition, but there is no electrical system; hence the headlamps are acetylene.

A cone clutch is employed, and the gearbox has three forward speeds and reverse, while final drive is by shaft. The wire wheels, which impart an extra rakishness to the car's appearance, have 710x90 tires all around. Brakes are on the rear wheels only, the footbrake on the transmission, and the handbrake on the drums.

The suspension is by rigid axles with semi-elliptic leaf springs at the front and by similar springs combined with a transverse leaf spring at the rear. The bodywork on this particular example of the 8-horsepower Clément-Bayard is more sporting than the standard tourer with its unusual fenders and headlamps. Driving accommodation is particularly good for the period, and the design ensured good weather protection.

The origin of the name Clément-Bayard is curious. Gustave Adolphe Clément, a keen French businessman who made a fortune in the bicycle and pneumatic tire industries in the late 19th century before founding the Clément make, appended Bayard to its name because one of his factories was in Mezières, a town delivered in 1521 by the Chevalier Bayard. He later also changed his own name with official sanction to Clément-Bayard.

The effigy on the hood of this car (left) is of the Chevalier Bayard who liberated the town of Mezières. The 8-horsepower Clément-Bayard combined mechanical simplicity with a high degree of comfort.

Amilcar 1100-cc

1926

The little French Amilcars were among the classic sports cars of the 1920s, although their fortunes soon faded. Several examples of the beautiful watch-like G6 six-cylinder, 1,100-cc model have survived intact, such as the one in the Grandson museum, while in England one or two still appear in vintage racing events. The production model "six" was, in fact, a road-equipped, super-sports car that could rapidly be adapted to pure speed races in the 1,100-cc class by removal of the fenders and lights and covering in the second, staggered, seat.

The car has an extremely advanced twin overhead camshaft, in-line engine with the diminutive bore and stroke of 56x74 mm and a total displacement of 1,093 cc. The supercharger, driven off the nose of the crankshaft, makes it credible that the production model has a power output of around 62 horsepower. The special factory team of racing Amilcars, which had special roller-bearing crankshafts and other modifications, gave 83 horsepower at 6,000 rpm, and that figure increased with continued development. The production model had an impressive maximum speed of 109 mph.

That lovely little engine has a single carburetor mounted on the supercharger, high-tension magneto ignition, and full pressure lubrication. Transmission comprises a single dry-plate clutch, four-speed gearbox and torque tube final drive. General construction of the car is very light, its total weight being only 1,430 pounds (650 kg), aided by the use of light alloys.

Suspension is by semi-elliptic leaf springs at the front and by quarter-elliptic cantilever springs at the rear. The braking arrangements, obviously adopted with racing in mind, are noteworthy, featuring large-diameter drum brakes on all four wheels with Perrot operation and a mechanical servo unit.

The normal road-axle ratio is 4.5:1. Rudge-Whitworth wire wheels with quick-release hubs carry 4.00x19 tires at the front and 4.40x19 at the rear. Wheelbase is 87 inches and the track 40 inches. Conforming with the times, the chassis is by pressed-steel longitudinal members with strong but light cross members riveted in place.

The exquisite little six-cylinder, twin-cam engine of the Amilcar 1100 looks compact enough to be a Four; only the number of exhaust pipes and plug leads give it away. Yet this engine was powerful enough to propel the car at no less than 106 mph, thanks largely to the supercharger.

Rolls-Royce
Phantom I

1927

The New Phantom or Phantom 1 had the shortest life of any of the classic models made by Rolls-Royce. Introduced in 1925, it was, in fact, withdrawn from production in 1929. It had been designed as the successor to the legendary Silver Ghost, but its sales cannot have been helped by the fact that it was launched on the market at the same time as the Rolls-Royce Twenty.

There is no doubt, however, that the Phantom 1 is an outstanding car, and the example in the Grandson museum, reputed to have belonged to film actress Greta Garbo, is a particularly fine specimen. It is an open "two plus one," and its torpedo lines are complete down to the air intakes, in the shape of marine ventilators, on the hood.

The engine is a huge 7,668-cc, in-line Six in two blocks of three cylinders with a detachable head. It has a bore and stroke of 108x139.5 mm. As is traditional with Rolls-Royce, the power output was not disclosed, but it must be in the region of 95 to 100 horsepower, with a maximum speed of 75—78 mph (120—125 kph). The overhead valves have pushrods and rocker arms, there is dual ignition by magneto and coil and a Rolls-Royce twin-jet carburetor with separate starting device. The oil pressure is regulated by the position of the accelerator pedal, and the engine is water cooled by a pump and thermosiphon, with hand-controlled radiator shutters. The cylinder head is cast iron while the sump is aluminum.

The flywheel incorporates a single dry-plate clutch, transmitting to a four-speed gearbox and propeller shaft, enclosed in a torque tube, to a floating rear axle. Suspension is by semi-elliptic leaf springs on the front axle and by cantilever springs at the rear, with adjustable shock absorbers on to all four wheels. There are drum

Above, the instrument-packed dashboard and the steering column with all main controls well within reach. The tiny windshield is in strange contrast with the size of the car. Below, the rear end of the strange wing-shaped runningboard in which the tools are housed.

brakes all around, with a mechanical assist, controlled by the gearbox.

The chassis is a bolted and welded steel structure with very sturdy side members, and the wire wheels of the car at Grandson are covered by disks; 7.00x21 tires are fitted. General dimensions are liberal, with a wheelbase of 144 inches, a front track of 57 inches, and rear track 1 inch narrower. Naturally such fine vehicles attracted the world's finest coachbuilders, with superb results.

VERKEHRSHAUS DER SCHWEIZ

The *Verkehrshaus der Schweiz,* or Swiss transport museum, which was opened on July 1, 1959, stands on the edge of the lake just outside Lucerne. Its modern buildings, which blend pleasantly into a background of green countryside, are all linked together so that the visitor can move from one to another, while remaining under cover all the time. A few of the exhibitis stand in the open air, however, as it is felt that boats or railway engines, for example, are best displayed outside.

This museum covers all types of transport and endeavors to trace their historical development. Land, water, and air transport all feature equally, and the visitor will find that coaches, trains, airplanes, ships, and even spacecraft, are on show, plus, of course, motor cars.

There is a fine selection of these, totaling about 30 and including some very rare specimens. In particular, these represent Swiss production in the early years of this century when Switzerland made important contributions to the history of motoring—a fact usually overlooked nowadays.

One of the first impressions given by this

museum is the excellent accessibility of the exhibits. All the vehicles displayed are arranged so that visitors can get close to them, and in some cases there are working models that can be put into motion by pressing the appropriate buttons.

As in every self-respecting museum, there are well stocked archives and a library where consultation is made easy, and a conference room able to accommodate up to 500 persons, and equipped for showing films.

Although vehicles and air and watercraft from other countries complete the panorama, the basic theme is to give the visitor some idea of the evolution of transport in Switzerland, where all means of carriage and communications, from sledges to satellites, are used.

The railway and telecommunications sections, for instance, are chiefly devoted to Swiss production, which is famous for being very advanced in this field. The section on navigation deals mainly with the development of lake communications, while that on aeronautics touches on all the nations that have made significant contributions in this field—those from Switzerland, incidentally, represent experimental projects which, though little known, are nonetheless extremely interesting.

Finally, the section dealing with road transport ranges from the first motor cars to the most recent, as well as covering other road vehicles such as the bicycle and the truck. Naturally the Swiss-made cars are of particular interest, since they are little known outside the country; they include the 1898 Popp, 1902 Berna (built by the concern that today manufactures heavy trucks), 1905 Dufaux, 1907 Turicum, 1908 Ajax, and 1919 Piccard-Pictet, plus chassis by Fischer, Saurer (another commercial vehicle manufacturer), Orion, and Martini.

There are also many fine foreign cars on view, while the huge trellis hung with a series of wheels is a most striking exhibit, illustrating the evolution of this essential element of land locomotion. The Swiss can boast of engineers and inventors of the first order in the field of motoring, and the fact that today they produce no passenger cars apart from the prestigious and very de luxe Monteverdi is due to economic considerations and certainly not inability.

Popp 7-hp
1898

Lorenz Popp, a designer living at Basle, built his first two cars in 1898 with the financial backing of Eduard Burkhardt, who was the agent for Benz in Switzerland. The Popp in the Lucerne museum is one of the pair, and thus it is not surprising to note that the car resembles the Benz Velo of a few years earlier, at any rate as far as appearance goes. However, the inventive genius of the designer ensures that the similarities are no more than superficial, for the mechanical elements are completely original.

The mid-mounted, water-cooled engine is a four-stroke with parallel twin cylinders mounted horizontally. The 92x120-mm bore and stroke give an engine capacity of 1,595 cc and the declared power is 7.6 horsepower. The inlet valves open automatically, but the exhaust valves, remarkably, are operated by a chain-driven overhead camshaft, which actuates the valves by means of L-shaped rocker arms.

Ignition on the car at Lucerne is by hot tubes, but it seems that an electrical system with battery and spark plugs was an alternative fitting. Transmission is by belts to a countershaft, the actual engine unit being slid along the chassis in guides by a lever, thus tensioning or slackening the belts to act as a clutch. Use of alternative pulleys provides two speeds and a reverse, and drive from the countershaft to the rear wheels is by chain. The change-speed lever is mounted on the vertical steering column, which has a notably small steering wheel.

The chassis of the 1898 Popp is unusual, comprising two longitudinal steel tubes joining the front and rear axles, with a chassis proper, also of steel tubing, mounted above and linked to the lower one by four fully elliptic leaf springs. The front spring supports of this "upper" chassis curve back to a near-vertical structure supporting a dash, two gas tanks, and the single road lamp. The brakes on the original car were simply two shoes which, when the pedal was depressed, applied direct to the rear

tires; these brakes do not appear on the car at Lucerne. Another unusual feature is the steering, which is by chain from a sprocket on the lower part of the steering column to a forward sprocket working a rack and pinion. The wire wheels, much smaller in front than at the rear, carry 55x650 pneumatic tires at the front and 80x945 at the rear. Chassis dimensions of this two-seater Phaeton are: wheelbase, 50 inches and track, 45 inches. Its speed was a claimed 25 mph (40 kph).

There are similarities in several details of the Popp and the Benz Velo, from which the Swiss designer must have drawn his inspiration. Both the suspension and the twin-cylinder engine differ, however.

Berna Ideal

1902

The Berna car preserved at the Lucerne museum is an early example of a make that still exists for the manufacture of commercial vehicles. There are strong indications that its makers were inspired by the little de Dion "vis-à-vis" of the period, for not only is the general layout much the same but also the influence of the French car is clear in several details, although the Berna differs in others. It seems certain, in fact, that Joseph Wyss, the founder of the Berna Company, was also in contact with other Swiss designers, such as Rudolf Egg.

This open tourer has a single-cylinder, water-cooled, vertical engine of Berna manufacture, mounted just in front of the rear axle. Bore and stroke are both 100 mm, giving an engine capacity of 785 cc, while the power output is 5 3 horsepower. The gearbox has two forward speeds but no reverse, and is in unit with the final drive.

Rigidly attached to the chassis, this gearbox was clearly inspired by the de Dion (or perhaps built under license) in that it consists of a system of constant-mesh gears (two pairs for the two gears), with one or the other of them being engaged by means of neat little friction

The seating arrangements on this Swiss car are interesting; the front seat is offset to the left so that the occupant will not impede the driver's view. Note the starting handle for the rear-mounted engine, jutting out under the driving seat, also the curious oval tiller.

clutches operating inside two drums. The two clutches are worked by a lever situated under the steering handle on the Berna. A maximum speed for the 880-pound car of 7.5 mph (12 kph) could be reached in first, and full maximum in second was 23.5 mph (38 kph).

The rectangular-plan tubular chassis has leaf spring suspension. The front axle differs from the usual in having three semi-elliptic leaf springs, two of them of normal longitudinal type, and the third transverse. It is bolted centrally to the chassis, and its outer ends are linked to the rear ends of the longitudinal leaf springs. Yet another de Dion feature is the rear axle, in which

articulated drive shafts give a measure of independence though tied by a cross tube, with advantages in low unsprung weight. Semi-elliptic leaf springs supply the suspension medium.

The car at Lucerne was registered in 1902 and still retains its original number plate. It has a three-seater body, built by Geiseberger; the driver and one forward-facing passenger occupy a bench seat, with another passenger facing sideways on a seat in front, set to the left to give the driver a clear view. Incidentally, the car cost 4,600 Swiss francs in 1902 and was guaranteed for one year.

Weber

1902

Weber was a Swiss make, founded in 1899 by Jules Weber of Uster, near Zurich, which built cars until financial difficulties put them out of the automobile business in 1906. The 1902 Weber to be seen at Lucerne has a rear-mounted, single-cylinder 1,652-cc engine of 165x100-mm bore and stroke. It is installed in a sturdy tubular steel chassis with semi-elliptic springing all around, and has an open body with curious seating disposition, the driver being well ahead the front wheels.

The most interesting feature of the car is undoubtedly the infinitely variable belt-drive transmission, as used on the Egg car seven years earlier (see page 201) and presumably adopted by Weber under license. The basic elements of the "gearbox," which anticipate that of the modern DAF from Holland, are two conical pulleys of variable diameter, connected by a belt. By means of a lever near the driver's hand, the diameter of one pulley can be increased while the other is reduced, so that the length of the belt remains the same, though the transmission ratio is altered.

Even more ingenious is the solution adopted to make this system work as a clutch too. A second lever allows the diameters of both pulleys to be increased or reduced at the same time, so that the belt is either stretched or slackened. In this way one pulley can be connected with the engine, which is started up while the car remains stationary, while the tension of the belt is gradually increased to take up drive. Once the car is under way, the transmission ratio is varied progressively until the most suitable one is found. A gear system is used for reverse.

Although earlier Webers were fitted with wire-spoked wheels, the example at Lucerne has wood-spoked artillery type, fitted with 815x105 tires at the front and 875x105 at the rear, both obviously oversize for the period and marring the authenticity of the car. The wheelbase is 61 inches and track 47 inches. Despite the advantage of their transmission over other cars of the day with noisy gearboxes and harsh clutches, Weber cars lost ground to their competitors and failed to progress further.

The curious variable-pulley transmission system patented by Egg was adopted under license on the Weber (opposite). The small steering wheel has two pegs to make driving easier for those used to a tiller.

Dufaux Racing Car
1905-07

Charles and Frédéric Dufaux started building cars in Geneva in 1904. Some sources of information indicate a possible early contact between the brothers and the Swiss Pic-Pic factory, even if, in fact, the latter began its activities when the Dufaux works had already produced a number of cars.

The racing Dufaux in the Lucerne museum is stated to be the 1905 type, although some believe it to be the later car built for the 1907 French Grand Prix. Whatever its exact age, it has been beautifully rebuilt and put into running order by Max and Charles Hahn, who have even tried out the car on the road to check its maximum speed, which they gave as 93 mph (150 kph).

Undoubtedly its most remarkable feature is the engine. At a period in racing when large four-cylinder units were the accepted practice, the Dufaux brothers plumped for an in-line Eight with 125x130-mm bore and stroke, and the formidable displacement of 12,760 cc. It developed between 100 and 120 horsepower at its maximum crankshaft speed of 1,300 rpm.

The cylinders are cast in four groups of two, with big bronze water jackets around each pair, giving the engine an unusual appearance, which suggests a massive Four. The side-by-side valves are all on the right of the engine, with inlet pipes grouped in pairs terminating in two carburetors, while the exhaust pipes are single for No. 1 and No. 8 cylinders, but paired for those in between.

Lubrication of this engine is by combined pressure and splash; the water cooling requires no less than 65 liters (over 17 gallons) of water in the imposing front-mounted radiator, while the cylindrical fuel tank mounted at the rear holds 100 liters (26.5 gallons) of fuel.

Apart from its vast engine, the Dufaux racing car follows the customary pattern of the day. Its chassis is formed of two long channel steel side members with curved front suspension supports and substantial cross members riveted in place. The body in front of the driver has a big cowling suggestive more of 1907 than 1905, while the two seats are fashioned in basket-work, perhaps for lightness or for the cool comfort of the occupants. The huge cast-iron flywheel contains the clutch, and the three-speed gearbox is separate from the engine and fixed to the chassis in unit with the differential on the crossshaft. The gearbox has two change levers, one engaging first and reverse, the other engaging second and third. Another lever operates the brakes on the rear wheels. Final drive is by side chains on massive sprockets.

Suspension is by semi-elliptic leaf springs on front and rear axles, and the wood-spoked wheels mount 815x105 tires on the front and 820x120 on the rear. The wheelbase measures 101 inches and the tracks at front and rear are 50 inches. In its day the weight of the straight-Eight Dufaux ready for racing was approximately 2,600 pounds; yet it had a top speed of almost 95 mph.

Even though the Dufaux engine looks like an enormous Four, there are, in fact, eight cylinders in four blocks of two each. Points to note are the fine execution of controls on the steering column, with well-finished brass sectors (above) and the friction shock absorbers (below).

Ajax Landaulet

1908

Ajax was a short-lived but very well-constructed Swiss car from Zurich, which first appeared in 1906 and was in production until 1910. Probably the finest model they ever made was the 8/16 Type A Landaulet, an example of which can be seen today at the Lucerne museum. Its elegance is reflected in its price, 15,000 Swiss francs, which was expensive even for 1908, and contributed to the demise of the make.

Its four-cylinder, side-valve engine is water-cooled, and the 85x100-mm bore and stroke give a total capacity of 2,270 cc and a power output said to be around 16 to 20 horsepower. With this power the car could attain 37 mph (60 kph), with a fuel consumption of about 12 liters per 100 km (roughly 20 miles per gallon). In the manufacturers' detailed description of the car's performance, even the oil consumption is given, stated as 0.4 liters per 100 kilometers (roughly 1 pint per 80 miles).

One of the characteristics of the engine is the huge flywheel incorporating a fan; it has vanes and a large recessed hub housing the multi-disk clutch, which operates in an oil bath. The customer had the option of chain or shaft drive; the latter system is featured on the car at Lucerne. A four-speed gearbox is employed.

Undoubtedly the most ingenious aspect of the Ajax is the mechanical starting system, which consists of a leverage device connected to the runningboard so that the weight of a man boarding the car was sufficient to produce enough rotary power to turn the engine over and start it. In 1908, the year the 8/16 was brought out, Ajax advertising boasted that its cars were simple and reliable, and as silent as if they were electrically powered. Meticulously and sturdily built, they were manufactured almost entirely within the factory at Zurich, even down to accessories, which were generally mass-produced by firms that specialized in such items. Several of the Type A Landaulets were used as taxicabs; the car at the Lucerne museum is an example. Its artillery wheels are fitted with out-of-period oversize tires, which spoil the otherwise impressively original condition.

The Ajax Landaulet weighs 3,100 pounds and could maintain a speed of 38 mph. The passengers in the enclosed rear section naturally enjoyed the greatest comfort, but at least the driver had no instruments to worry about—to judge from their total absence from the dashboard, anyway!

Fischer Torpedo

1913

Martin Fischer (1867–1947), a Swiss designer who began his career as a watchmaker, was one of the most prolific inventors and constructors of his time. The 1913 Fischer car exhibited in the Verkehrshaus der Schweiz at Lucerne is his last successful model, for a six-cylinder engined car he brought out in 1914 proved too cumbersome and heavy for the tastes of the public and soon after the start of World War I, his factory closed.

Under a rather conventional exterior, the Fischer 33CV Torpedo conceals some unusual and admirable technical features. The in-line, four-cylinder, sleeve-valve engine, the gearbox with internally toothed pinions—both Fischer patents—and also the quick-change wheels

with their center-lock fixing and single central nut were all well ahead of the standard equipment of the day.

The engine is water cooled, and there are two half-moon-shaped semi-sleeve valves to each cylinder. These elements slide axially in the cylinder and are actuated by internal cam-wheels and right-angled connecting links. The cam-wheels are on two shafts driven by gearing from the crankshaft, which runs in five bearings. Bore and stroke are 85x120 mm, giving a total engine capacity of 2,723 cc and a maximum power of 33 horsepower, which is developed at 1,200 rpm.

Ignition is by a Bosch magneto, and fuel is gravity-fed to the carburetor, while the lubrication is a mixed sys-

tem of splash and forced feed. A multiple-plate clutch transmits the drive to Fischer's remarkable patent gearbox. This consists of a large-diameter drive wheel having four internally-toothed gear "steps," and connected with the final drive propeller shaft. The shaft from clutch to gearbox is universally jointed and carries a pinion able to engage with any of the four gear "steps" by use of the gear lever, thus providing four forward gear ratios. For reverse there is a second pinion that comes into position between the engine pinion and the first-gear teeth. This unusual internally toothed gear train is embodied in the Fischer radiator badge.

The chassis of this car is completely conventional, with pressed-steel, C-section side members, and semi-elliptic leaf springs on both front and rear axles. The footbrake works on the transmission, and the handbrake on the drums of the rear wheels. Wooden-spoked artillery-type wheels are fitted, on which are mounted 3.5x30 tires. Lighting is by acetylene, with the generator on the runningboard. Wheelbase of the Torpedo is quite long at 132 inches; the track measures 53 inches.

Top left, the acetylene gas generator for the headlamps is precision-made in brass. Bottom left, a glove compartment in 1913. Right, the radiator badge illustrates two Fischer innovations—the internally toothed drive gears and half-moon-shaped semi-sleeve valves.

Pic-Pic

1919

This car's curious name is derived from the Société Piccard-Pictet et Cie, a Geneva-based engineering company formed by two partners, Piccard and Pictet, who in 1904 were entrusted with the manufacture of SAG cars. These were high-quality luxury products designed by the engineer Marc Birkigt, later of Hispano-Suiza fame. Pic-

card-Pictet continued to turn out SAG's vehicles with every satisfaction until 1910 when, unfortunately, the company was closed down.

The partners thereupon decided to set up as car manufacturers themselves; they had the facilities and the experience, and the Pic-Pic was the result. It was a very well-made and durable make of car in the SAG tradition, which was built until 1920 and which enjoyed an excellent reputation for dependability during World War I.

The 1919, 15 CV model to be seen at the Lucerne museum was carefully restored by the motor vehicles section of the Swiss Army, which itself was once equipped with Pic-Pic cars. It is a large, six-seater "torpedo" (tourer) with a conventional chassis that has pressed-steel side members, well cross-braced, and rigid axles with semi-elliptic leaf springs.

Its most interesting feature is undoubtedly the single sleeve-valve engine of Burt-McCollom type built under license from the Argyll Company of Glasgow, Scotland. In each of the four cylinders there is a sliding sleeve with holes aligning with the combustion chamber. The cylinder walls, too, have holes in them, which correspond to the inlet and exhaust ports. By means of both a rotary and axial movement, the holes in the sleeve are made to

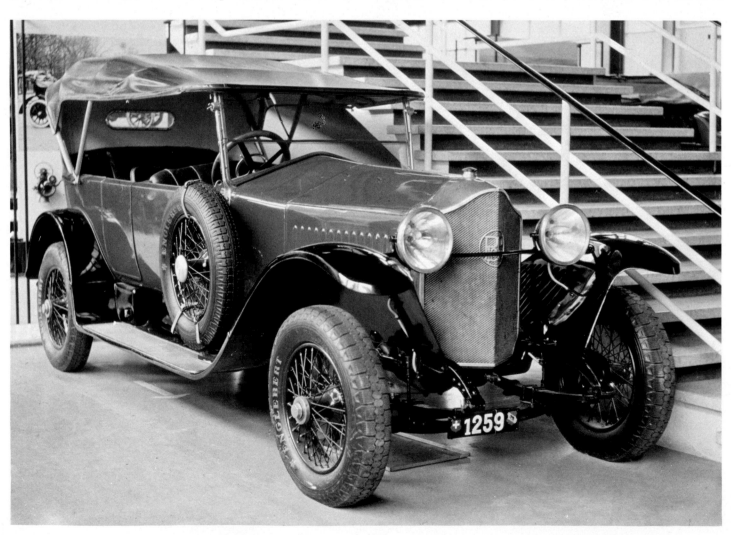

The dashboard of the Pic-Pic rivals those of Rolls-Royce in the precision of workmanship and number of instruments. Performance of this solidly built car, which scaled 3,500 pounds, is good, with a maximum speed of 55 mph. Pic-Pics were used both by the Swiss Army, and for racing.

coincide alternately with the port in the cylinder opposite the inlet, then with those opposite the exhaust.

Bore and stroke of the engine are 85x130 mm, giving a total displacement of 2,950.5 cc, an output of 50 horsepower at 1,800 rpm, and a healthy maximum speed of 56 mph (90 kph). The car is fitted with a multiple-disk clutch, and the four-speed gearbox is in unit with the engine. Transmission to the rear wheels is by open drive shaft. The footbrake works on the transmission, and the handbrake on the rear wheels. The Rudge-Whitworth wire wheels are today fitted with 880x120 tires, which are clearly oversize for the period, marring the accuracy of the restoration. But there is no denying that the workmanship and design in this elegant Swiss car was among the best of its period.

BRIGGS CUNNINGHAM
AUTOMOTIVE MUSEUM

Great sportsmen generally concentrate on one particular sport, and if they extend their activities to another, it usually has some connection with the first. Briggs Cunningham is an exception, for one cannot easily associate motor racing and sailing—the two sports in which he excelled. In motor racing he placed extremely well in various races, including the world-famous Le Mans 24-Hours, driving cars that he himself had manufactured, while in sailing he had the coveted honor of successfully defending the America's Cup.

For one with such a passion for cars, able to afford to collect and preserve them, it was a logical move for Cunningham to amass a collection of sports cars of all ages and to found a museum to house them. His fine collection began about thirty years ago, when several extremely valuable cars were acquired. His original concept of a collection of sports cars—that is, two-seaters with outstanding performance but suitable for use in normal road conditions—was widened when he decided to add a number of historic racing cars to his fleet.

The predominance of European makes

in the Cunningham Museum is easily explained when it is realized that the sports car is a European concept, and only in Europe have large numbers been manufactured. Thus examples of the Bugatti, Bentley, Hispano-Suiza, Ferrari, and Cicitalia are to be seen; but one must not forget the American Duesenberg, Mercer, and Cunningham's own Cunninghams, which have battled honorably on foreign soil, challenging European supremacy at the beginning of the 1950s, when it seemed unassailable.

The cars, many of them retrieved in bad condition, have been carefully restored by a team of experts and put into running order. They are displayed in a modern building covering an area of more than 4,800 square yards. Most of the cars on display belong to the private collection of Briggs Cunningham and his wife, Laura (who is herself an experienced racing driver), but sometimes cars on loan from other collections are shown.

Altogether there are over 70 cars dating from 1911, plus many classic engines and chassis, while other cars are in reserve or being restored. Not only are almost all the cars extremely rare pieces (for example, the Bugatti Royale, only seven of which were ever built), but also many are significant for their feats in racing, such as the 1914 Mercedes and the 1927 Grand Prix Delage, while others are important as forerunners of technical progress; the 1913 Grand Prix Peugeot is a classic example, much copied by American and other European makers.

The Briggs Cunningham Museum stands in the little town of Costa Mesa in California, 40 miles south of Los Angeles, and not far from the sea and the main road. The famous California climate, with its eternal spring, might have been made for the regular outdoor exhibitions, *concours d'élégance,* and driving tests for owners of veteran cars, which are frequently organized on the museum grounds.

A kind of club has also been formed by the museum for vintage and veteran enthusiasts, who are able to keep in touch, receive technical and historical information, and make detailed examinations of any particular car on display. This is an unusual but welcome development, providing evidence of the ever-growing interest in historic motoring.

Mercer 35T
1912

The Roeblings were a family of enthusiastic motorists who began to make cars at Trenton, New Jersey, in 1910. A year later they launched the Mercer 35T, better known as the Raceabout, one of the United States' most famous early sports cars.

The example in the Cunningham Museum is in superb condition. The Raceabout is an orthodox but carefully built car that could be used both for racing and normal driving, and this was the secret of its great popularity. It has a large, four-cylinder, T-head engine with side valves operated by two camshafts, one on each side in the crankcase. The bore and stroke are 110x120 mm, giving a total displacement of 4,789 cc. A sturdy, sweet-running unit, it developed 55 horsepower at 1,650 rpm, and the maximum speed of a Raceabout was a guaranteed 70 mph, although many authorities claim a genuine 75 mph.

The engine is water cooled with a centrifugal pump driven off the timing gears; the shaft also carries the fan. Adequate lubrication is assured by about 8.5 quarts (8 liters) of oil in the engine sump, circulated by a gear-driven force-feed rotary pump. Ignition is by Bosch magneto and twin spark plugs to each cylinder, placed opposite the valves. There is a Fletcher double-jet vertical carburetor, which is fed with gas from the rear-mounted tank by a gear-driven pump.

The engine and gearbox are separate, but share an independent sub-frame mounted within the main chassis, which is composed of pressed-steel, open-section longitudinal members and central cross-bracing. Suspension of the two rigid axles is by semi-elliptic leaf springs with Hartford friction shock absorbers all around. Internal expanding drum brakes work on the rear wheels, but there is a pedal-operated band brake on the transmission and a handbrake to the wheel drums.

Great care was taken to ensure that the driver is firmly seated at the car's top speed of 75 mph; there are bucket seats and also a form of external stirrup into which the right foot is inserted to work the accelerator. A hand throttle is fitted on the steering wheel, together with the ignition control.

With its monocle windshield, rakish fenders, and spare wheels behind the big bolster gas tank, the Raceabout had a personality all its own. About 500 of these striking cars were built, but no more than 20 survive.

Typifying the classic sporting Mercer is its great central mobile headlamp, later imitated by other makes, and the monocle windshield mounted on the steering column.

Pierce-Arrow 48 Roadster

1915

During its 29-year life span, the name Pierce-Arrow stood for top quality in the United States and also, for a certain time, in Europe. Springing in 1909 from the older Pierce make, the cars were built in Buffalo, New York; in 1928 the Studebaker Corporation took the firm over, only to resell it to financial interests in Buffalo five years later.

The 1915 Roadster in the Briggs Cunningham Museum is in impeccable condition. The 48 in its title refers to its fiscal horsepower, but the huge 8.6 liter engine is capable of developing a much higher output—about 70–75 horsepower at the maximum limit of 2,500 rpm, with a superbly smooth, silent tickover at only 150 rpm.

The engine is composed of three blocks of two cylinders each, with 114.3x139.7-mm bore and stroke. Displacement is 8,600 cc. Each block is integral with its head and has side valves; there are two spark plugs per cylinder with two independent distributors for dual ignition. The carburetor is of Pierce-Arrow manufacture, with automatic compensation of the mixture by both the accelerator pedal and hand throttle.

Lubrication is by pressure to all crankshaft and connecting rod bearings, and the cooling system comprises a

pump and a fan. The sump, inlet manifold, and gearbox casing are all of aluminum, as are many parts of the bodywork. Surprisingly for this late date, the leather-covered cone clutch was fitted with an oil bath; yet the car has a completely electric lighting system with generator and large-capacity battery, and the four-speed gearbox boasts a pre-selection system. The headlamps mounted on the front fenders are a unique Pierce-Arrow feature first introduced in 1915.

The frame is a sturdy but conventional structure with two pressed-steel side members and cross-bracing. The forged steel front axle is suspended by semi-elliptic leaf springs and the semi-floating rear axle has three-quarter elliptic springs. Two braking systems act on the drums of the rear wheels—an external contracting handbrake and an internal expanding foot-brake. The wooden, artillery-type wheels mount 35x5 tires, the wheelbase is a majestic 142 inches, and the fuel tank of this imposing carriage holds no less than 26.5 gallons.

By 1915 special headlamps merging into the front fenders giving a streamlined effect were a Pierce-Arrow feature. Its roadster-type body might be called a forerunner of the modern two-plus-two.

Bugatti Type 41 Royale

1927

The Golden Bug has passed into the field of legend, together with its illustrious maker, Ettore Bugatti. Only six of the Type 41 were built in as many years, but they were the finest that could be achieved in luxury, comfort, and styling, even if somewhat impractical, for accounts of the day mention the difficulties encountered in negotiating sharp bends with a car that had a wheelbase of no less than 169 inches.

The engine is a vast monobloc straight-Eight, and although the prototype, built in 1926, measured 125x150 mm, giving an engine capacity of about 15 liters, subsequent Royales had a 125x130-mm bore and stroke, giving a total displacement of 12,763 cc. The power output is in the region of 300 horsepower at only 1,700 rpm; in its construction this engine is a bold essay in advanced engineering.

The cast-iron cylinder block is in one with the head and the crankshaft bearings, creating an immensely rigid whole with little possibility of stress or distortion. This block carries aluminum casings, which enclose it, retain the cooling water, and form the sump. There are three valves per cylinder—two inlet and one exhaust—driven by a single overhead camshaft, and although maintenance is at long intervals only, it is necessary to strip the whole engine down in order to remove the valves for grinding! Such problems would not trouble potential owners of the Bugatti Royale, however, because it was intended for royalty and wealthy connoisseurs.

Ignition is both by magneto and by coil and battery, with two spark plugs to each cylinder, while fuel feed is by electric pumps and a vast Guattti-built twin-choke carburetor with the mixture preheated in the manifold. The clutch is separate from the engine, which is mounted in the middle of the chassis (under the front seat) in an aluminum housing. The gearbox is built in one with the rear axle and has only three speeds—a low starting gear, a direct-drive second, and a high indirect top.

Contemporary reports give the Royale's maximum speed in direct drive as 93 mph (150 kph) and 124 mph

This car, with its 12.7-liter engine and enormous size, is held by many to represent the very acme of power and luxury. Despite its dimensions it had a certain agility, and certainly beauty. Note the subtle balance of curves in the front view (right), and how the graceful shapes of the axle, radiator, and fenders form a harmonious whole.

(200 kph) in top at 2,000 rpm. The chassis is extremely strong, its side members measuring 10 inches deep in the center. Suspension is by semi-elliptics at the front and by two pairs of quarter-elliptics at the rear. The huge, light alloy wheels are cast in one piece with the brake drums, and the car at Costa Mesa has 7x24-inch tires. The car, which once belonged to Bugatti's daughter Ebé, has a superbly proportioned body by Kellner of Paris.

Cadillac 452B

1930

The Cadillac V-16 was one of the finest and most-coveted of American cars in the early 1930s. Its 7.4-liter engine, although by no means the largest ever encountered in a car, has the greatest number of cylinders ever on a private car. Bore and stroke are 76.2x101.6 mm, giving a total displacement of 7,413 cc. The two blocks of eight cylinders are set at 45 degrees on an aluminum crankcase. Overhead valves are operated by pushrods and rocker arms from a single camshaft in the center of the vee, and both inlet and exhaust manifolds are mounted outside the blocks.

Carburetion is by a single, vertical-barrel instrument to each bank. Both the crankshaft and the camshaft run in five bearings, and the former is what was termed a compensated crankshaft and has a front-mounted harmonic stabilizer. With a 5.3:1 compression ratio, the engine could develop 165 horsepower at a crank-

shaft speed indicated as between 3,200 and 3,400 rpm. Torque and general operation are extremely smooth, thanks to the large number of cylinders.

Ignition is by 6-volt Delco-Remy coil with a dual distributor, which is nourished by an enormous 130 amp/hour battery. Water cooling is by pump and fan, with a thermostatic control to open or close the radiator shutters as temperature demands. The lubrication system includes a pump, filter, and a reserve of almost 10 liters (10.5 quarts) of oil in the sump.

Transmission is via a dry twin-disk clutch and a typical American gearbox with three forward speeds and reverse, although such is the torque of the 16-cylinder engine that these need not be heavily used. The drive shaft is enclosed in a torque tube, with spiral bevel final drive and three-quarter floating rear axle.

The frame of the V-16 Cadillac is naturally a sturdy

Antoine Laumet, a Frenchman, founded the town of Detroit in 1701 and changed his name to the high-sounding Monsieur de la Mothe Cadillac. He could not have foreseen that the name would later become famous—as a car!

affair, with deep pressed-steel side members, amply cross-braced. Suspension is by semi-elliptic leaf springs at front and rear, which are metal-encased for protection, while hydraulic shock absorbers are fitted.

Mechanically operated drum brakes with vacuum-assist are fitted all around, and although the bodywork as represented by the example at the Cunningham Museum typifies the American car of the period, the 146 inches wheelbase of the car gives it added elegance. The whims of the owner led to this car having a special compartment for carrying golf clubs, modified internal accommodation, and oversize 20-inch tires.

Stutz Super Bearcat
1932

With its Bearcat and Super Bearcat models, the Stutz Company of Indianapolis, Indiana, tried to establish an American sports car that was clearly inspired by European examples. The car in the Briggs Cunningham Museum is a 1932 Super Bearcat with short chassis and "bobtail" convertible body. It is of particular interest as Stutz's last private car design.

Its engine is a magnificent straight-Eight with twin overhead camshafts and four valves per cylinder, two inlet and two exhaust. Bore and stroke dimensions are 85.7x114.3 mm, giving a total capacity of 5,277 cc and producing 156 horsepower at 3,900 rpm. A speed of over 100 mph was claimed for the car. Cooling is by water, centrifugal pump, and fan, while the radiator shutters are thermostatically controlled.

The nine-bearing crankshaft is pressure-lubricated, and the twin camshafts are chain-driven. A Schebler Duplex carburetor is fitted, and ignition is by coil and distributor with a 6-volt electrical system. Both clutch and three-speed gearbox are conventional, and the semi-floating rear axle has underslung worm final drive. The drive shaft is open, the thrust being taken by the springs—that is, Hotchkiss-type drive.

The Super Bearcat's frame is extremely sturdy, with two deep, thick longitudinal members (at their center point they measure 7.8 inches deep and 2 inches wide). There are also five transverse members. Suspension is

Its short wheelbase (105 inches) gives the straight-Eight twin-cam 5.2-liter Stutz Bearcat a purposeful appearance. It was one of the United States' fastest sports cars in the 1930s.

by semi-elliptic leaf springs on both axles, with Gabriel hydraulic shock absorbers. The very effective brakes are hydraulically operated on all four wheels with vacuum-assist.

Typifying the early 1930s era are the Stutz's wire-spoked wheels with large-diameter hubcaps. The two-seater body with external luggage compartment, rear gas tank, and extra luggage grid, looks extremely short. Indeed, the wheelbase is only 105 inches, which is 20 inches shorter than the normal Bearcat model. Track is 56 inches (front) and 58 inches (rear).

The body was the work of Murray, the American coachbuilder, using the well-known Weymann system of construction in which a flexibly jointed wooden framework is employed; in the case of the Stutz, supporting aluminum panels were used. The two spare wheels are carried in the sweep of the front fenders, as was the popular fashion at the time.

Despite the fact that Stutz undeniably built cars of high quality and performance, like other de luxe makes they were doomed to disappear with the Depression.

Packard Twelve

1933

For many years the Detroit-built Packard was the proud possessor of a reputation for quality and elegance that could bear comparison even with Rolls-Royce. In an era of large, luxury 12- and 16-cylinder engined rivals, Packard introduced their much revered Twelve. Produced between 1931 and 1934, it is a car that was practically handmade and sold with what in practice were special bodies. Indeed, only 2,000 specimens of this model were built, and any surviving today, like that in the Briggs Cunningham Museum, are cherished for the true classics they are.

The twelve cylinders are in two banks of six, forming a 60-degree V, and have a bore and stroke of 87.3x101.6 mm, giving a total displacement of 7,300 cc. Maximum output is 160 horsepower at 3,200 rpm on a compression ratio of 6:1, and maximum speed was declared as 100 mph.

The V-12 cylinder block is cast in a ferrous alloy with a high nickel percentage; the detachable heads are flat since the engine has side valves. The crankshaft runs in four, broad white-metal main bearings, and the sump is of cast aluminum.

Cooling is by water, with a centrifugal pump and belt-driven fan, plus a thermostat controlling the opening of the shutters on the distinctive and handsome vee radiator characteristic of the Packard. There is copious pressure lubrication to all engine parts, including the piston little ends, with special control of the oil temperature. Ignition is by distributor and twin coils, the

This was a great car for state processions and tours, with a second windshield for the rear seats, useful when traveling with the top down as a support during official parades, or just when motoring fast to keep the wind off the passengers—highly essential with a 100 mph maximum, thanks to the Packard's superb 7.3-liter, 12-cylinder engine.

electrical system is 6-volt, and carburetion is by a large Stromberg instrument.

Transmission on the 12-cylinder Packard comprises a twin dry-plate clutch, a synchromesh gearbox with three forward speeds and reverse, and a freewheel with mechanical servo operation. Propeller shaft final drive is to a semi-floating rear axle. The chassis follows conventional pattern with pressed-steel side members, but these are cross-braced by a sturdy X-shaped transverse member.

Suspension is by semi-elliptic leaf springs to both front and rear axles, and there are drum brakes to all four wheels, the handbrake working on the rear wheels. The wire wheels carry 7.50x17-inch tires with the popular white sidewalls. The superbly elegant phaeton in the Cunningham Museum has the longer of two wheelbase options at 146 inches, and weighs just over 4,700 pounds.

Cunningham C-6R

1954

It is natural that, among the many fine cars in the Briggs Cunningham collection, several places had to be reserved for those manufactured by Cunningham himself. It was the determined aim of this great sportsman to take part in that classic, European, long-distance sports car race, the Le Mans 24-Hours, with an entirely American car, and this he succeeded in doing in the years 1950 to 1955.

Of the seven Cunningham cars to be seen at the museum, the 1954–55 C-6R is the most recent and clearly shows the cumulative experience of its designers. It is low, clean, and compact, unlike its forebears. Its tubular chassis has independent suspension at the front,

with wishbones and large coil springs, a De Dion-type rear axle, also with coil springs, and hydraulic telescopic shock absorbers fitted all around.

In reaction, perhaps, to earlier Le Mans Cunninghams, which were rather heavy, the C-6R weighs only 1,852 pounds, of which the open two-seater body, built in Jaguar D-type style, accounts for only 198 pounds. Unfortunately, gearbox trouble forced the car's retirement from the 1955 Le Mans race.

The engine used in this race was a Meyer-Drake Offenhauser, that famous American four-cylinder racing unit of prodigious output, with many years of Indianapolis 500 race development and many victories behind it. As modified for the Cunningham it had a 100.8x92-mm bore and stroke, a capacity of 2,942 cc, and was adapted to run on gas instead of methyl alcohol, using two Weber two-barrel carburetors. With an 8:1 compression ratio it developed a good 270 horsepower at 6,000 rpm, but after the failure at Le Mans this engine was replaced by a 3.8-liter Jaguar six-cylinder unit. It is in this form that the car can be seen today at Costa Mesa. The engine drives through a Borg and Beck multi-plate clutch, a four-speed, all-synchromesh ZF gearbox, and a limited slip differential in the final drive. Lockheed hydraulic brakes with 13-inch diameter drums are fitted, and the cast alloy wheels carry 6.50x16-inch tires.

Wheelbase of the Cunningham C-6R is 100 inches and the front and rear track is 52 inches. Although not the most successful of the Cunningham sports racing

cars, the C-6R is representative of a make that, though it never won Le Mans outright, gained several honorable places there.

The resemblance to the famous D-type racing Jaguar is obvious in this American car, which reflects the style of an era not long superseded.

Maserati Type 60
1961

Engineer Giulio Alfieri, chief designer of Maserati at Modena since 1955, has given much proof of his ingenious and unorthodox interpretations of competition car design. Undoubtedly the works he will best be remembered for are the Type 60 and 61 two-seater sports racing cars with the multi-tubular frame, which earned them the nickname Birdcage.

This English name was given to the series of Maseratis that began with the Type 60, which was introduced in 1959 in 2-liter form and was followed by 3-liter Type 61 versions a year later. All these employed a revolutionary space frame with a network of small-diameter tubes welded together to form a rigid and extremely light structure. On average the Birdcage frame was claimed to be half as light as the conventional chassis of the period, but with increased torsional rigidity, and, in fact, the 1961 2-liter Model 60 in the Cunningham Museum has a weight of only 1,290 pounds (585 kg).

The front-mounted engine is canted to the right at an angle of 45 degrees to allow the hood to be kept very low; it is a water-cooled, in-line, four-cylinder unit with twin overhead camshafts and valves inclined in the hemispherical combustion chambers. Twin Weber two-barrel carburetors are used, and lubrication is on the dry sump principle, with separate oil cooler.

With a bore and stroke of 93.8x72 mm, giving 1,989 cc and running on 100 octane fuel, the power output is 200 horsepower at 7,800 rpm on a 9.8:1 compression ratio. A maximum speed of over 165 mph was claimed for this car. Transmission is through a multiple dry-plate clutch and a five-speed gearbox, in unit with a limited slip differential, on the rear axle. The Birdcage chassis has independent front suspension by coil springs, wishbones and an antisway bar, while a de Dion-type rear axle is used, suspended by a transverse leaf spring. There are telescopic hydraulic shock absorbers all around.

Dunlop disk brakes, hydraulically operated, are fitted on all four wheels, and the quick-release wire wheels mount 5.60x16-inch tires at the front and 6.00x16-inch at the rear. The bodywork can best be described as functional without being beautiful; it has a low nose for minimal frontal area, and a high tail, which contains the fuel tank and on which is mounted a sturdy roll bar to protect the driver in the event of accident.

Although very much more a racing car than a true road sports machine, Cunningham's 2-liter Maserati

Birdcage has a complete electrical system in accordance with Le Mans 24-Hour Race requirements; it took eighth place outright in 1961, driven by its owner, Briggs Cunningham himself, and Jim Kimberly.

The unusual, somewhat ungainly shape of the body results from the need to cover the mechanical elements while keeping external dimensions down to a minimum. The result is an 1,290 pounds, 2-liter, 165 mph car.

HARRAH'S AUTOMOBILE COLLECTION

In his superb museum in Reno, Nevada,
William (Bill) Harrah has gathered together
one of the largest automobile collections in
the world. He has close to 1,500 cars of historic value, over 1,000 of them on display
in a vast 10-acre complex that also houses
aircraft, boats, and many objects of interest from the period between the middle
and the end of the 19th century.

It would be hard to calculate the total
value of the collection, since restoration
costs would have to be added to the pur-
chase price of the cars, which are often
bought in deplorable condition. It seems
reasonable to guess their fortunate owner
has spent about three million dollars on
them, and he keeps about 140 specialists at
work on the restoration and preservation
of the collection.

Bill Harrah himself is one of the most
skillful businessmen in the United States,
ranging from hotels to the sale of automobiles (he is the Ferrari distributor for the
western United States). His main source of
income, however, is gambling—he owns
some of the most famous casinos in Reno.
The automobile collection forms part of his
tourist center, since visitors to the museum
are attracted to the casinos and vice versa.

The collection was started in 1948,
when Harrah bought a couple of old cars,
a Maxwell and a Ford, both dated 1911,
and then another two right afterward,

But several years went by before it grew to any great size, and Harrah became aware of its importance and possibilities.

This happened around 1953, and from then on the orders were always to buy. In fact, Bill Harrah's agents bought all the old cars of any note that came to light, even if they were examples of models already in the collection. Thus there are dozens of cars of the same type in Harrah's ownership; but even if they are not all on show the duplicates still have value, and serve as reserves or to exchange for other cars.

One may wonder why Bill Harrah goes on adding to his collection beyond any apparent practical or commercial advantages. His museum is already an established tourist attraction, and would be if there were only five hundred rather than fifteen hundred cars on show. He is no lover of personal publicity or interviews, but he did grant one once, admitting he cannot resist old cars, particularly if they are in bad repair. Buying and restoring them is to him a worthwhile task and gives him a great deal of satisfaction.

Only a few minutes from the center of Reno, the collection is displayed in a series of old warehouses which have been handsomely renovated. The main building holds the most important part of the collection, and there is also a smaller building with cars; then the collections of a non-motoring nature, and finally the section devoted to restoration. This last is both surprising and highly interesting, using as much space, machines, equipment and tools as a model automobile factory. Here any car of any period can be rebuilt or repaired. Harrah does not work on the cars himself, but he keeps a jealous watch on their progress and tries out every car to make sure the restoration is successful.

A library with an enormous number of catalogues and manuals relating to every possible make of car has been organized to facilitate this work, for most makes which have been in world-wide production are in the collection, some of them extremely rare and costly. Outstanding examples include a Bugatti Royale, over a dozen Rolls-Royces, Marmons, Duesenbergs, and so on. There are over 90 Packards alone, a dozen Mercers, seven Mercedes including an SSK, and three Isotta-Fraschinis, to give an idea of the quality and quantity of the Harrah museum's contents.

There seems to be greater emphasis on American makes, which would obviously be more obtainable; the early period is not as well represented since most of the cars are later than 1910; 19th-century cars are few and far between. Those that are included are extremely well worth seeing, however, and in magnitude and quality the Harrah Automotive Collection is truly staggering.

Thomas Flyer

1907

This is the actual car that won the famous speed and endurance race from New York to Paris in 1908, covering more than 12,400 miles. They started from New York on February 12, drove west across the United States in the heart of winter, went by ship to Japan and then overland through Siberia to Europe. As had Borghese's Itala in the 1907 Peking-Paris race, the Thomas Flyer left its adversaries (except the heavily penalized Protos) way behind, reaching Paris on July 30 with an enormous lead over the only other competitor still in the race.

The Thomas Flyer was a production car, for the American decision to enter the race had been made hastily. The choice fell on one of the two models being sold in 1907 by the Thomas Company of Buffalo, New York—the Type 35, which had a very strong in-line, four-cylinder engine with 146x139.7-mm bore and stroke and a total displacement of 9,369 cc. The power declared was 70 horsepower, and maximum speed was about 60 mph. Water cooling is by pump and fan, there is mixed type lubrication, and, to guarantee starting in all circumstances, dual ignition is by magneto and coil.

There is a multiple-plate clutch and separate four-speed gearbox, transmitting to a transverse final drive with differential, and side chains to the rear wheels. The extremely sturdy steel chassis has semi-elliptic leaf spring suspension on both axles. The front axle is the only component not used on normal production Thomases; permission was given by the organizers of the race to replace it with one that was flat-based instead of radiused, in order to raise the lowest point of the car, giving it added ground clearance. The wooden-spoked wheels are all the same size, but are fitted with 36x4-inch tires at the front and 36x5-inch at the rear.

The other modification made to the car was on the bodywork. The normal fenders were replaced for the race by two broad guards 12 inches wide and 2 inches thick; these ran the length of the car and were useful to heave it out of the mud. Canvas splash guards were also fitted, an auxiliary fuel tank was added, and weight was given as 3,950 pounds.

As can clearly be seen (extreme left and below), one of the headlamps on this historic Thomas is still minus the glass, which was broken when a bird smashed against it during the crossing of Siberia. Above, note one of the special oilers on the side of the seat for the drive chains.

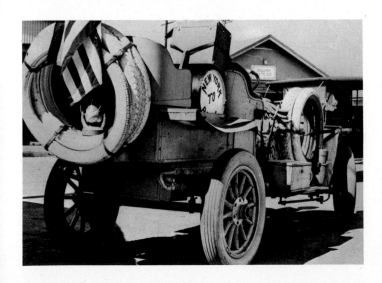

White Type O
1909

The White Sewing Machine Company, later the White Company, built some of the United States' finest steam cars up to the beginning of World War I, when gas-driven cars had long ceased to be a novelty. The firm still exists today, manufacturing heavy diesel-powered trucks. The five-seat, steam-powered model O was the smaller of two variants produced in 1909, but in everything except size it was a replica of the larger version.

The steam generating plant is a very low and wide tubular boiler, set under the rear seat. As it was a flesh

The steam power unit somewhat resembled its gas rival, with the condenser taking the place of the normal radiator. Outwardly, too, the car itself was not unlike a gasoline-engine contemporary.

boiler with instantaneous vaporization, there was no danger of explosion, for there was never more than a small quantity of water in it. The supply of fuel and the jet of water were automatically regulated according to the needs of the engine. This unit, placed under the hood, is of compound type with two vertical double-acting cylinders; the high-pressure cylinder has a 63.5-mm bore, while the low-pressure cylinder bore is 108 mm; the stroke is 76.2 mm in both. Maximum output is quoted at 20 mph.

The crosshead is made like the piston of a normal engine, and the connecting rods are cast in a single piece and mounted on ball bearings, as is the two-bearing driving shaft. The valves are operated by the

extremely simple and efficient Joy system, which allows power to be regulated and movement to be inverted by shifting the guide for the valve levers; the same control operates the water pumps.

All the mechanical parts are enclosed in the lower part of the sump in an oil bath and are easily accessible for repair. One great virtue of a steam car is that neither clutch nor gearbox is necessary, and the shaft drive on the White is direct to the rear wheels. The water tank is located under the floor at the front, and the fuel tank is set at the rear.

The armored wood frame has a stout cross member for the steam power unit, and suspension is by semi-elliptic leaf springs of normal type to both front and rear axles. The condenser for the engine is set forward and is designed to resemble a normal radiator, and there is a fan to increase the airflow.

Wheelbase of the White model O is 103 inches and the track 55.5 inches. The wheels are of wooden-spoked type, carrying 32x3.5-inch tires all around. The handbrake acts on the drums of the rear wheels by means of internal wedges, with the brake pedal acting on external bands.

Steam cars such as this White ran very much more smoothly and quietly than gasoline-engine vehicles, but were heavy and became increasingly expensive to manufacture as the years passed. White itself switched to internal combustion gas engines in 1911.

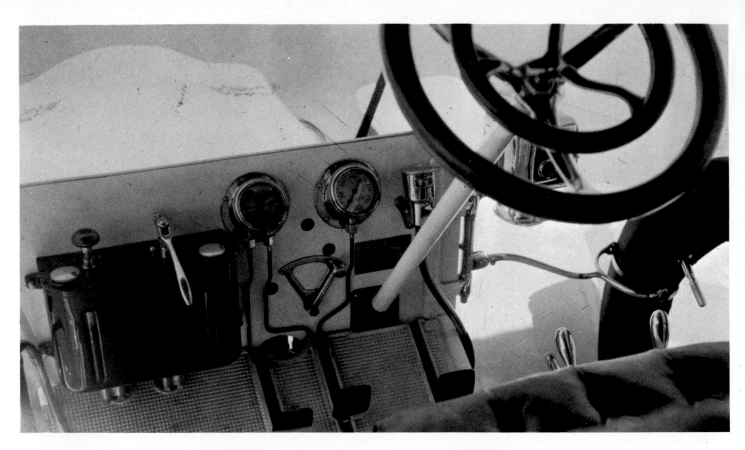

Winton 17B Tourer

1911

Alexander Winton, a Cleveland bicycle manufacturer, grasped the importance of the motor car as soon as he saw the first horseless carriages; in 1897 he became one of the first to start serious manufacture in the United States. He was also a pioneer of various side activities, from racing to the organization of the industry. The final destiny of his firm was to become part of General Motors, producing marine engines.

The 1911 17B tourer at the Harrah museum has interesting details, such as the use of a compressed-air system for starting the engine and inflating tires.

Its huge 48-horsepower, 7,819-cc engine has six cylinders in line, cast in blocks of two with side valves; the bore and stroke measure 114.3x127 mm, and the car could attain a speed of approximately 50 mph. The dual ignition with high-tension magneto and coil is typical of American practice right from the first years of the century, for the need to be able to rely on the electrical system to make full use of the car had long been appreciated. This Winton is water cooled, with a pump and honeycomb radiator. Drive from the front-mounted engine to the rigid rear axle is by a disk-type clutch, four-speed gearbox, and shaft.

The chassis is extremely sturdy, with a massive

The two extra folding seats can be seen (top left). The special Firestone tires with the tread reading "Non Skid" were a feature of the time, when the Winton was a typical American quality car.

forged front axle and conventional semi-elliptic leaf spring suspension features both at front and rear. The wheelbase is 124 inches and both tracks are 56 inches. The brakes are on the rear wheels only, controlled by lever and pedal. The 12-spoke wooden wheels are all the same size and are fitted with 36x4.5-inch tires.

The open touring body (a limousine was also manufactured on the Winton 17B chassis) has a folding canvas top and two folding seats, which are quite comfortable, in addition to the regular seating, so that up to seven or eight passengers could be accommodated. The divided windshield, with the lower part steeply angled, gives the car a particular personality, which is accentuated by the division of the rear window in the fold-down top into eight parts. This particular Winton car was originally owned by the late George C. Pardee, governor of California.

The Maxwell factory in Detroit, Michigan, was one of the results of the wave of enthusiasm that swept the United States for the new form of horseless transport. It was founded in 1904 under the name of Maxwell-Briscoe, but in 1912 the second partner, Briscoe, broke away and the make was bought up by Walter Flanders, continuing under the single name of Maxwell until 1923, when it was absorbed by Walter P. Chrysler to launch his own make of car.

One of the slogans of Maxwell was "Perfectly simple, simply perfect," and its staple products were straightforward, reliable, and unexciting. The most popular models had four-cylinder side-valve engines, but one example in the Harrah Collection is a rarer in-line Six, perhaps the only one of 1914 type that has survived.

The fine 6,242-cc engine, of 104.8x120.7-mm bore and stroke, developed 50 horsepower. It has a Rayfield

It can fairly be said that this Maxwell represents the typical American touring car of its day, with swept fenders, wooden wheels, and high, spacious build. It has full electric lighting and starting.

carburetor and dual ignition by magneto and coil, the latter with a dry battery. The side valves, set to one side of the cylinder block, are operated by a single camshaft in the crankcase. Cooling is by water, with radiator, pump, and fan.

Transmission follows the conventional pattern, with a three-speed gearbox in unit with the engine and a shaft to the semi-floating rear axle. The robust chassis has steel C-section side members with cross-bracing, the usual

semi-elliptic leaf spring suspension at the front, and three-quarter elliptics at the rear.

The Maxwell 50-6 has wooden-spoked wheels, fitted with 36x4.5-inch tires all around. It is a lengthy car, as can be seen from the 129-inch wheelbase; both front and rear tracks are 55 inches. The exceptional length of the chassis allowed a very roomy body to be fitted, with accommodation for no less than seven passengers, two on the front seat, two on folding seats, and three on the rear seat. Despite having an open body, the car was rather heavy, weighing about 3,900 pounds when dry. Its top speed being no more than about 43 mph.

Pierce-Arrow Type 41

1931

When the Type 41 was built, the Pierce-Arrow make was part of the Studebaker Corporation, the American factory that had won fame in the 19th century with its production of Conestoga wagons for the pioneers, and had then moved on to manufacturing cars in 1902. Pierce-Arrow itself began as the Pierce in 1901, subsequently becoming one of America's great prestige makes. It was the luxury member of the Studebaker stable, and the Type 41 in the Harrah Collection is a typical example; it is a large, powerfully engined car of great elegance.

Its engine is a side-valve straight-Eight with 88.9x127-mm bore and stroke, giving an engine capacity of 6,306 cc, and a maximum speed, in impressively smooth silence, of about 87 mph. The compression ratio is 5:1, and the power developed is 132 horsepower at 3,000 rpm. Fuel feed is through a Stromberg vertical carburetor, and all the elements of the water-cooled engine are pressure lubricated. The completely counterbalanced crankshaft turns in nine main bearings, and the engine block is of cast iron. There is a single dry-plate clutch, and the four-speed gearbox is in unit with the engine. Transmission is by shaft to a hypoid bevel rear axle, and both the gearbox and the final drive are made by Pierce-Arrow itself.

The Type 41 chassis was built in two different lengths, one with an 140-inch wheelbase, the other with 146-inch wheelbase, which permitted really spacious and elegant bodywork. Suspension is by semi-elliptic leaf springs all around; the wire wheels with their fashionable large-diameter hubcaps mount 7.00x18-inch tires and have mechanically operated drum brakes to all four wheels, with the handbrake acting on the rear wheels.

The four-door body, called a Custom Club Sedan and built by the famous American coachbuilder Le Baron, is set centrally on the chassis, virtually providing inter-axle seating, and is completed by a neat separate luggage compartment, which gives the car a character of its own. The front end is dominated by the superbly elegant chromed radiator with thermostatically controlled radiator shutters, and by the unique headlamps with the casings merging directly into the fenders—a recognizable Pierce-Arrow feature for many years. Cam and lever steering helped to make this large, heavy car handle sweetly and with great precision.

Although from the front this car may seem chromed to excess, the treatment is effective on the big Pierce-Arrow. Above, right, the curious faired-in headlights that are typical of the make. The large rear gas tank (right) looks alarmingly vulnerable despite the deep chromed bumper bar. This big 132-horsepower car could reach 87 mph.

Bugatti Type 50T

1932

Few names excite the car connoisseur more than Bugatti, those exquisitely engineered creations designed by a great artist and son of Italy who became a citizen of France. To take the place of the Bugatti 46S in 1930 came the glorious Type 50. At first chassis and transmission were the same as on the earlier model and only the engine was new, but then with the presentation of the 50T, the whole car was renewed by use of a longer chassis (the T, in fact, stands for Touring).

The greatest innovation of this make was undoubtedly the introduction of twin overhead camshafts operating valves inclined at 45 degrees in a fixed head. One theory is that Bugatti copied this system from the American Miller racing car, two examples of which he had acquired in 1929. The eight cylinder, in-line, water-cooled engine has a bore and stroke of 86x107 mm, giving a total displacement of 4,972 cc; it has a large super-

charger, and develops around 200 horsepower at 4,000 rpm.

Two American Schebler carburetors supply air and fuel mixture to the supercharger, coil ignition is employed, and lubrication is of the wet sump type. The timing system is rather complicated, comprising a vertical shaft driven off the crankshaft via a pair of bevels, which in turn drive the oil pump, water pump, supercharger, and a train of five pinions to the double camshafts. The multiple dry-plate clutch is inside the flywheel, which is mounted on a rubber joint that acts as a buffer and vibration damper. The three-speed gearbox is integral with the rear final drive, as on the Type 41 Bugatti Royale.

The 50T's chassis has pressed-steel side members and a typical Bugatti interpretation of non-independent suspension. The front axle is a forged and elegantly shaped

As far as its shape is concerned, this is one of the most unusual, if not eccentric, of the Bugatti bodies. The 50T model was also one of the most luxurious. The wooden dashboard (left) is crammed with instruments. Above is shown one of the friction shock absorbers, adjustable from the driving seat by means of a flexible cable.

tube with semi-elliptic leaf springs, while the rear axle-cum-gearbox is carried by reversed quarter-elliptic springs; both axles are controlled by friction shock absorbers adjustable from the driver's seat.

Very handsome cast aluminum wheels are fitted, these having fins for the ventilation of the brake drums, which are integral with the wheels; 6.50x20-inch tires are fitted. The wheelbase is 122 inches and track 55 inches. The unusual body, with its exaggerated slope to the windshield, has decided aerodynamic pretensions and stamps the car with unfailing Bugatti personality.

De Soto Airflow Six
1934

The De Soto was an offshoot of the Chrysler Company, and when the parent concern introduced the unusual streamlined 4.4-liter eight-cylinder Airflow in 1934, they added a De Soto version with 4-liter, six-cylinder engine. A rare two-door survivor of the De Soto Airflow has been preserved by the Harrah Collection.

The lines of these cars were very bold for 1934, with the short, broad hood merging with the fenders, and headlamps faired into the bodywork; structurally, too, the car was revolutionary. It was an early American attempt at unit construction of chassis and body, in which the body shell contributed decisively to the rigidity of the whole.

Such importance was attached to structural strength that there were only relatively tiny openings for access to the engine, with side hatches in the wheel arches to get at some of the most important components. This made maintenance very difficult and was probably one of the reasons why the Airflow model was abandoned in 1937.

The engine is set well forward, allowing roomy inter-axle accommodation for six passengers on the two bench-type seats; the vee windshield is in two sections, which can be opened separately. The six-cylinder, side-valve, water-cooled engine has a cast-iron block and aluminum head, and a bore and stroke of 85.7x114.3 mm, giving a total capacity of 3,954 cc, and developing 100 horsepower gross at 3,400 rpm. There is pressure lubrication and ignition by battery and coil. A cross-flow radiator is set low behind the curved, streamlined grille and has a thermostat.

Transmission is through a single dry-plate clutch and three-speed gearbox integral with the engine and shaft final drive, while there is a free-wheel device which can be locked at will. Wheelbase of the De Soto Airflow two-door is 114 inches; the brakes are hydraulic.

Other technical subtleties that make this car more interesting than its average American contemporary are the electric automatic device for supplying a richer fuel mixture and the automatic system for adjusting the temperature of the intake manifold.

The Airflow body was a serious attempt, not only at aerodynamic lines, but also at semi-integral construction. Besides this De Soto model, other versions appeared under the Chrysler nameplate, some with four doors.

Auburn 851 SC Speedster
1935

The Auburn's large, flexible exhaust pipes are chromium-plated, while the tail tapers away like a racing boat; these are distinctive features of the somewhat showy American sports car of the 1930s. The words "Super-Charged" distinguish this model from the normal version.

A sports car in America in the 1930s more often than not meant an Auburn. The model 851 SC Speedster in particular (SC stands for Super-Charged) had the added fascination of being blown by a centrifugal compressor with a clutched drive system giving a 6:1 ratio compared with the speed of the engine. Thus when the engine reached its maximum crankshaft speed of 4,000 rpm the compressor was turning at 24,000 rpm!

The engines were made for Auburn by Lycoming, and the blown version, of which a superb example in rich red is to be seen in the Harrah Collection, developed 150 horsepower as compared with the 115 horsepower of the unblown model. The engines of both types were basically identical, except that the higher boost supercharged versions were more carefully balanced.

With a bore and stroke of 77.78x120.65 mm, the straight-Eight unit has a capacity of 4,590 cc. The cylinder block is of cast iron, the head of aluminum, and the compression ratio is 6.5:1. Valves are side by side, and the engine has coil ignition and pressure lubrication. The drive is taken through a conventional clutch and three-speed synchromesh gearbox in unit with the engine and a drive shaft to the rear wheels.

Quite normal, too, is the chassis with its pressed-steel side members and semi-elliptic leaf springs for front and rear axles. The brakes are hydraulically operated, and the drums have a diameter of 12 inches, unusually large for those days; the handbrake acts on the rear wheels only. Handsome disk wheels carry 6.50x16-inch tires, and the maximum speed was guaranteed to be in excess of 100 mph.

Although only a two-seater, the Auburn Speedster has a lengthy chassis with a wheelbase of 127 inches and front and rear tracks of 59 inches and 62 inches respectively. Its length allowed the body designer to give the car a handsome pointed tail, and with its deep, valanced helmet-type fenders and the four flexible outside exhaust pipes on each side of the hood, the Speedster has a striking appearance. It is a ruggedly built, heavy car, however, scaling 3,700 pounds dry and over 3,900 pounds curb weight.

HENRY FORD MUSEUM AND GREENFIELD VILLAGE

Henry Ford was born on a farm at Dearborn, near Detroit. Today, Dearborn is the heart of the vast Ford empire, and here stand the various buildings of the Ford Technical Center, a pleasant hotel in the colonial style, and the Ford Museum, with its annex, Greenfield Village.

It was in September 1928 that Thomas Edison laid the foundation stone of the Museum, and today the buildings illustrating the history of the United States cover practically 200 acres of land. Greenfield Village has several historic buildings, some being copies of the originals, while others have been literally dismantled and rebuilt in the Village.

The Ford Museum itself is a large building in pure colonial style, which not only sets out to illustrate the customs and traditions of the American way of life, but also its technological development, for which Henry Ford's enthusiasm was unbounded.

It would take days to make a thorough inspection of all the sections of the museum. There are collections of every kind, reproductions of craftsmen's workshops of earlier centuries, rare pieces such as one of the first machine guns with a rotating barrel, and one of the famous Conestoga pioneer wagons.

The land and air transport section is the richest, for no effort and certainly no expense would have been spared to hunt out and acquire significant exhibits. The aircraft exhibit naturally includes one of the famous Ford Tri-Motors, and there is a fascinating series of railway engines, including the largest and most powerful in the world.

The motoring sections form one of the most extensive and important collections of historic vehicles ever assembled. It comprises several hundred vehicles, although not all are exhibited at one time. All the vehicles displayed are in near-perfect condition, thanks to careful restoration or, in many cases, to the fact that they were acquired when in a fairly new state, and thus suffered no neglect or deterioration.

Many exhibits are unique, such as the Selden, the car built by the lawyer who in the early 20th century claimed a royalty from everyone in the U.S. who was making automobiles on the grounds that he had patented the very concept of an engine-driven vehicle. Since it was Ford who fought and won the legal battle against Selden's claim and thus freed the industry from a heavy burden, it is appropriate that Selden's vehicle should be on show. There are also American steam and electric cars—at least fifty of each kind—and about a hundred gas-driven cars. Ford vehicles are naturally well represented: there is an example of each of the important models made by the company.

Many of the exhibits have added interest because of the duties they performed; for instance, the Lincoln used by King George VI during his visit to the United States, one of Kaiser Wilhelm II's cars, one belonging to J. Pierpont Morgan, and an armor-plated Lincoln used by the Presidents of the United States.

The multitude of exhibits makes the museum somewhat crowded, but it attracts an enormous public and the organizers do everything they can to encourage visitors. Books and photographs on various subjects are on sale, and this is certainly one of the most complete automobile museums in the world.

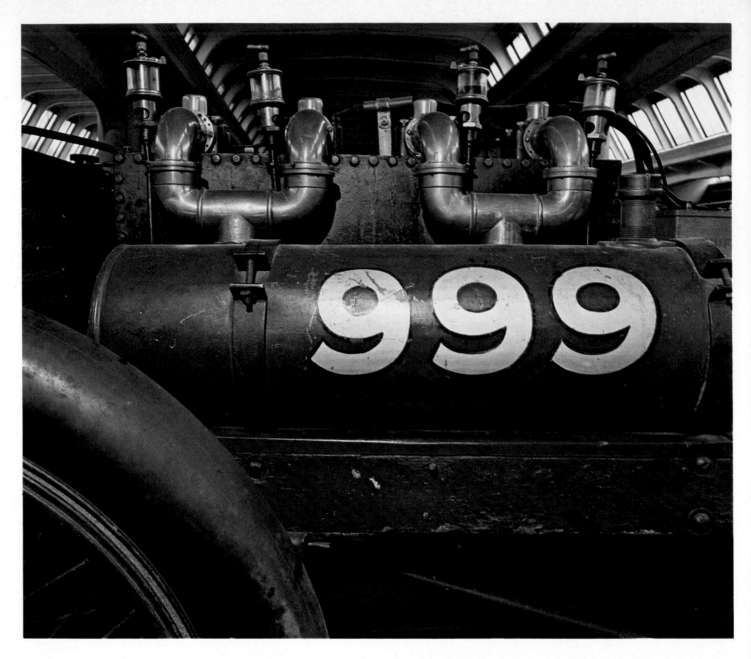

Ford 999

1902

In 1902 Henry Ford, who took an almost reluctant interest in racing during the heroic years of motoring, decided in the interests of publicity that he would have to build a really fast racing car. In fact he built two, which he called 999 and the Arrow, but which were more or less the same. The only one still in existence, however, is the 999 in the Ford Museum.

It is a rather unsubtle, rudimentary car even for its day, but its only purpose, at a time when Ford was striving to make his name, was to travel fast enough to show how good the make was. The huge, four-cylinder, in-line engine is mounted in a chassis formed from a pair of longitudinal wooden members, with steel plating on the front half, and cross members. The 184.15x177.8-mm bore and stroke and 18,950-cc displacement are dimensions that have only been exceeded by record cars of later years. The engine turned over at

between 800 and 850 rpm, and its power is given by the historian H. O. Duncan as 52 horsepower, although other sources state that it is 80 horsepower.

There is neither gearbox nor differential, for the engine ran all the time in direct drive, and the clutch consists of a wooden block expanded against the inside of the flywheel—an enormous affair with a diameter of 2 feet and weighing 240 pounds, which spun close to the

A practically brakeless mechanical monster, scarcely resembling a car, yet able to exceed 90 mph—that is how the Ford 999 can be defined. Above can be seen the exposed bevel gears of the final drive to the unsprung rear wheels, also a rudimentary band brake.

driver's legs. The suspension, too, is reduced to the minimum, figuring only at the front in the form of two small semi-elliptic springs; the rear axle is clamped direct to the side members of the frame.

Steering is by a kind of two-handled tiller arrangement of which, legend has it, Henry Ford once said that it would also serve to show the driver when the car was running in a straight line if he couldn't see for the dust! The famous Barney Oldfield drove 999 to victory in several races in the early days of American racing, while Henry Ford himself drove the Arrow on a frozen lake in January 1904, breaking the world speed record at 91.37 mph, a figure unrecognized by the authorities.

Ford
Model A

1903

When Henry Ford formed his own automobile manufacturing company in 1903, he called his cars by the letters of the alphabet. Thus the first model from the new production became the Model A of 1903, which was followed by others less well-known until we come to the legendary Model T, which made Ford's fortune. Not every letter denoted another model; some were assigned to prototypes that never saw the light of day. When Ford neared the end of the alphabet, he began all over again, so that there are two Ford Model As, separated by an interval of twenty-five years.

The 1903 Model A, an important exhibit at the Ford Museum, is characteristic of the period and does not stand out from its contemporaries in the way the Model T was later to do. In fact, not only was the same coachbuilder responsible for the bodywork of this Ford and that of the Cadillac of the same year, but the design of the Model A Cadillac also bore considerable Ford influence.

The Ford's horizontally opposed, twin-cylinder, underfloor engine is set lengthwise in the center of the frame with the crankshaft parallel with the axles, so

This was the first quantity-produced Ford, and the first to bear the letter A. It differed little from other American cars of the period.

that the starting handle is inserted from the side of the car. With a 114.3x101.6-mm bore and stroke and a total displacement of 2,085 cc, the power was about 9 horsepower at 900 rpm. Ignition is of the high-tension type with trembler coils, cooling is by a finned tube radiator, and lubrication by drip-feed oilers.

The gearbox is of epicyclic type, with two forward speeds and reverse, a system that was very popular in the United States and is clearly a forerunner of the Model T gearbox. Drive from the gearbox to the differential on the rear axle is by a single central chain. 28x3-inch tires are mounted on the wooden-spoked wheels.

Suspension on the Model A is unusual in having fully elliptic leaf springs both at front and rear, which are U-bolted centrally on their upper members to the metal chassis. The body wraps neatly around the chassis members, completely concealing them; it is of open four-seater type and is called a tonneau, having a rear door for access to the back seats. The use of a steering wheel instead of a tiller was an innovation for Ford, who favored the latter on his earlier prototypes. The car, which has a 76.5-inch wheelbase, weighs 1,280 pounds and was capable when fully extended·of reaching a maximum speed of about 25 mph.

Oldsmobile Curved-Dash Runabout

1903

The world's first mass-production motor car was the Oldsmobile runabout, which was built in the early years of the century and was called the Curved-Dash because the front part of the runningboard was turned up like the runner of a sledge. It was an extremely simple and reliable machine and was produced by a firm that later merged with others to form General Motors.

The 1903 example in the Ford Museum differs only slightly, and in minor details, from the models that preceded and followed it. One of the great merits of its single-cylinder, horizontal, rear-mounted engine was its relative silence, due to the low revs and a huge muffler. The cylinder has a 114.3-mm bore and 152.4-mm stroke, giving a displacement of 1,564 cc.

At 700 rpm the engine develops 5 horsepower, and the two gears of the epicyclic gearbox allow speeds of 7.5 mph in bottom and about 18 mph in direct drive to be attained, when the engine is revolving at about 760 rpm. Cooling is by water, and lubrication by gravity; there is high-tension trembler coil ignition with a control switch, and even the inlet valve is mechanically operated by the camshaft. This was unusual at a time when automatic suction operation still prevailed. The carburetor has a special vibrating valve that regulates the passage of gasoline according to the amount of air taken in.

Drive from the gearbox to the rear axle is by a single chain, and steering is by a tiller connected direct to the steering rods. Two braking systems both act on the transmission, the handbrake working on the final drive, the footbrake on the gearbox. The simple buggy-type frame

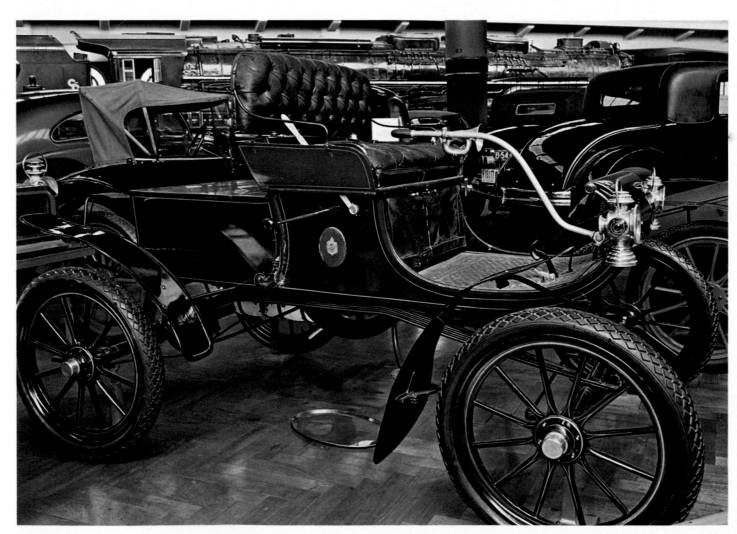

This delightful little American open tourer, the first to go into mass production, has full-length leaf springs, one end suspending the front axle, the other the rear axle. The design was simple, the product reliable, and thus the Curved-Dash was a resounding success.

takes the form of a small central rectangle supporting the engine, with two full-length longitudinal leaf springs, one one each side, with their respective ends acting as cantilever springs supporting the front and rear axles.

The wooden-spoked wheels carry 3-inch tires. Various sources give two different measurements for the wheelbase and tracks; in one case, a 69-inch wheelbase and 48-inch tracks, and in the second, the wheelbase is given as 67 inches, while the tracks are 47 inches. As more than one model was available, it is possible the dimensions varied.

Several thousand Curved-Dash Oldsmobiles were manufactured between 1901 and 1905.

Ford Model T
1909

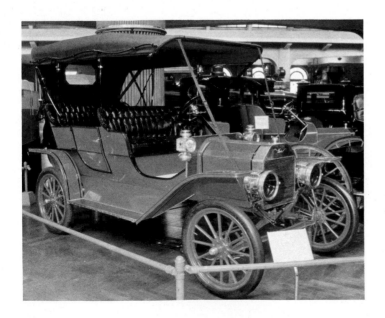

The most famous car in the world had extremely simple but sound suspension, as can be seen. The various components are smaller than might be expected since, even as early as this, Henry Ford was employing special tensile steels, which gave strength yet kept the weight down to 1,500 pounds (for the tourer). The maximum (and cruising) speed was 40 mph.

"The automobile that motorized America," as the Ford Model T has been called, was an ingenious blend of simple yet advanced design, of fine materials and economically planned production. Henry Ford wanted to make a reliable, trouble-free car in an age when the motor car was still a complicated and unreliable plaything; to this end he used the finest materials—for example, chrome vanadium steel—and simplified the design as far as was humanly possible to make driving and repairs easier, and to keep production costs down.

The monobloc four-cylinder, in-line, side-valve engine has a 95.2x101.6-mm bore and stroke and a displacement of 2,892.7 cc. The head is detachable, and the compression ratio, like the maximum power and revs, varied little during the 19 years' life of the Model T. In the 1909 example illustrated here, the power is 20 horsepower at about 1,600 rpm, with a top speed of about 40 mph. The single carburetor, generally of Holley or Kingston make, is gravity-fed from a gas tank located under the front seat. Ignition is by low-tension flywheel magneto with separate trembler coils for each cylinder (contained in a wooden box on the dash); water cooling is by the thermosiphon system and fan; and there is splash lubrication, with oil circulated by the flywheel, both to the engine and a very compact two-speed planetary gearbox, which shared the same oil.

Henry Ford's Tin Lizzie is justly renowned for being extremely easy to drive, thanks to the simplicity of the controls. Three pedals and a lever to control the two-speed epicyclic gearbox sounds complex but is straightforward. The lever, in the first part of its course, releases the clutch, and in the second part actuates the drum brakes on the rear wheels, while it has a fixed central position for neutral and starting. If the left-hand pedal is pushed forward it engages bottom gear, and if let right back it engages top, while halfway it is in neutral.

The center pedal controls reverse through a band clutch (and reverse could always be used as an extra brake) and the pedal on the right controls a band-type transmission brake on the drum of the direct drive

clutch. The system was such that by stamping on any two of the pedals the car could be brought to a halt. The accelerator and the spark advance are controlled by two levers on the steering wheel, and there is an epicyclic reduction gear in the steering column itself.

Final drive is by propeller shaft enclosed in a torque tube and straight-tooth bevel gears. The suspension is simple and rugged, with transverse leaf springs all around. The wheelbase is 100 inches and the track 56 inches, and the wood-spoked wheels have 3.5x30-inch tires.

Stanley Steamer
1910

The Stanley was one of the finest makes of steam cars, and the one that remained in production longest. One of the reasons for its popularity, apart from the excellence of the vehicles, was probably the world land speed record set at Daytona Beach, Florida, by Fred Marriott in a very special streamlined Stanley Steamer in 1906, at the breathtaking average for the time of 121.57 mph (195.6 kph).

Most of the wide range of steam cars built by Stanley through the years had the same basic characteristics—a tubular boiler, at first under the seat but later under the hood, and an engine set longitudinally in the frame. The 1910 car in the Ford Museum is one of the more modern examples, with a simulated front hood concealing the boiler. Its 10-horsepower engine is the smallest of the Stanley range, a double-acting two-cylinder unit, with a 76.2-mm bore and 101.6-mm stroke, giving a total displacement of only 927 cc. As is natural in a steam car, the steam pressure feed counted more than the dimensions of the cylinders, and in the production cars this was about 34–40 atmospheres or about 28 horsepower maximum.

The engine is under the floor and fully enclosed, and is connected directly to the differential of the rear axle by a pair of spur gears, the axle/engine group forming a single unit, with the front end of the engine attached to the frame by a flexible trunnion mounting. The power unit is completed by water and oil pumps and various manometers and safety devices, which by 1910 were already at a high level of efficiency.

A persistent Stanley problem was the water supply, for while the kerosene fuel used to generate the steam gave an average range of 155 or so miles, the water tank only held enough for about 50 miles.

The main engine controls are on the steering column, and both footbrake and handbrake operate on the rear wheels. The chassis is composed of two hickory side members, with fully elliptic springs on both axles. The wheelbase is 54 inches and the runabout could reach 31 mph.

The chassis of the Stanley Steamer was pared down to the bare essentials; the fully-elliptic springs were U-bolted direct to the simple wooden frame, and the slender axles were reinforced by full-length tension rods. This car could reach 31 mph, but heavy water consumption was a snag.

Franklin Airman

1928

Franklin was the great exponent of air-cooling in the United States from the first decade of the 20th century; it was renowned for its individuality and quality. The 1928 Airman sedan in the Henry Ford Museum used to belong to the famous aviator Charles Lindbergh, and is a misleadingly conventional-looking car with many unusual features.

The in-line, six-cylinder engine has an 82.6x120.7-mm bore and stroke, with a 3,874-cc displacement, and an N.A.C.C. (fiscal) rating of 25.35 horsepower at 1,700 rpm. The engine is air-cooled by a special system of centrifugal fan, scoops, and baffles; the six separate cylinders have vertical cooling fins and are completely shrouded by a metal casing within which the air is circulated.

Valves are overhead, operated by pushrods and rocker arms, the crankshaft runs in seven bearings, and lubrication is by pressure, with a gear pump that sends oil to individual bearings by a series of pipes. Coil and distributor ignition is by the Atwater-Kent radio firm, and there is a special Franklin carburetor.

Transmission is through a single dry-plate clutch and three-speed gearbox, the gate layout reversing the classic American scheme in that bottom gear is down to the right, second up to the left, and third back down. Front suspension is by semi-elliptic leaf springs, but at the rear fully elliptic springs are employed—a time-honored Franklin feature—in conjunction with a rigid rear axle that has semi-floating drive shafts.

The Airman was the first Franklin to use an all-steel chassis in place of the armored wood type favored for so long, and the first to have front wheel brakes, which shows how conservative the makers were. The Lockheed hydraulic internal-expanding type brakes were advanced for the time, however. So were other details, such as the device for enriching the mixture for starting, which was electrically controlled from the dashboard.

The wire wheels on the car in the Ford Museum were an option to the wooden-spoked type fitted as standard; the tires are 6x30 inches, and the wheelbase measures 122 inches. Weight was approximately 3,800 pounds (2,200 of that accounted by the engine), and the maximum speed around 52 mph. Franklins were always of high quality and were not cheap. Sales dropped progressively and the last were built in 1934.

Styling was the dictator, even in 1928, and although the air-cooled Franklin did not need one, it has what looks like a radiator.

N.J.—'33.
I 292

Duesenberg J
1931

The Duesenberg, one of the most glorious American makes of the late 1920s and early 1930s, was the work of an outstanding engineer, Frederick Samuel (Fred) Duesenberg, who vied with W. O. Bentley in his love for high-performance cars. Duesenberg cars reached the height of technical perfection and were owned by royalty, Hollywood stars, and business magnates.

The Model J, a superb example of which is in the Henry Ford Museum, has a straight-Eight, water-cooled engine with four overhead valves to each cylinder, which are operated by chain-driven twin overhead camshafts. Bore and stroke dimensions are 95x120.5 mm, giving a 6,882-cc displacement; the head is detachable and has hemispherical combustion chambers. With a compression ratio of 5.2:1, the gross power developed is 265 horsepower at 4,200 rpm.

A Schebler two-barrel carburetor is used; ignition is by 6-volt Delco-Remy coil and distributor, with two independent coils that each nourish four spark plugs. Pressure lubrication is extremely thorough, and the sump holds 6 quarts of oil. Interesting details are the mercury-filled vibration damper on the finely-balanced five-bearing crankshaft, and the aluminum connecting rods and pistons. A double dry-plate clutch transmits the power to a three-speed gearbox, and thence by torque tube-enclosed drive shaft to a hypoid bevel final drive.

Very few cars could match its acceleration figure of 0−100 mph in 21 seconds; this is backed up by an impressive maximum speed of 118 mph by a car scaling well over two tons.

The Model J has hydraulic brakes with large-diameter drums. The chassis is of channel-section steel, dropped between the axles, and with six tubular cross

The J's powerful straight-Eight, twin-cam engine almost fills the long hood, and its gross output of 265 horsepower drove the car along at up to 118 mph. The elegant lines made small concession to superfluous decoration, and even with the whitewall tires it is a dignified car.

members, while the suspension is by semi-elliptic leaf springs at front and rear, damped by Delco-Remy hydraulic shock absorbers.

The car in the Ford Museum is the "short" model with a wheelbase of 142.5 inches; the longer version, able to take spacious limousine bodywork, had a wheelbase of 153.5 inches. The tracks at front and rear measure 56 inches, and center-lock wire wheels carry

7.00x19-inch tires. Bijur automatic chassis lubrication was one of the Duesenberg's many special features; it was actuated every 75 miles.

The instrument panel is peerless. On the dashboard there is a fine clock and altimeter besides all the usual instruments, and there is also a manometer for pressure in the braking circuit and diverse warning lights anticipating modern instrumentation. No expense was spared in Duesenberg President Eric L. Cord's dream of offering "the finest thing on four wheels," and these magnificent cars and the even more powerful supercharged SJ were marketed until 1937.

Lincoln Model K

1939

Henry Ford purchased the ailing Lincoln Company in 1922, only two years after the make was launched, and set out to establish his new acquisition as one of the top quality American luxury cars. Lincoln sedans have, in fact, often been featured on official occasions in the United States.

In 1932 a new V-12 cylinder engine of 7.3 liters was introduced by Lincoln, and in slightly smaller form this unit was manufactured for several years to power their Model K prestige cars. One of the last examples of the car is preserved at the Ford Museum; it has a bore and stroke of 79.4x114.3 mm and a displacement of 6,791 cc.

Its two banks of six cylinders are set at 67 degrees, and the engine has aluminum cylinder heads, a 6:1 compression ratio, and side valves. It develops a maximum output of 150 horsepower at 3,400 rpm, permitting a speed of as much as 95 mph despite substantial weight.

Cooling is by pump and a large radiator, concealed behind that very handsome vee grille; the specification also includes coil ignition, single-barrel carburetor, pressure lubrication, and a four-bearing crankshaft, which helps to make a notably compact engine.

Transmission is through a single dry-plate clutch, the usual American-type gearbox with three forward speeds and reverse, and a torque tube enclosing the propeller shaft to a spiral bevel final drive. The rear suspension is unusual, having a transverse leaf spring (as on the old Model T), with two lateral arms to locate the axle. The front suspension is by normal semi-elliptic leaf springs. Wheelbase of the longest chassis, used for ceremonial cars, is no less than 145 inches, whereas the standard model is 136 inches. Braking is hydraulically operated, this feature having been introduced to the Lincoln range the previous year, and the wheels are wire type, mounting 7.50x17-inch tires. The car is distinguished by its two spare wheels, one on each side set in the front fenders, and by its headlamps built into the front fenders.

The royal coat of arms can be seen above the windshield of this car, which was used by H.M. George VI when he came to the United States.

Tucker Torpedo
1947

The Tucker project has one of the most staggering histories of the early post-World War II period of motoring. In 1947, when the whole world was wanting cars, Preston Tucker announced his plan to build a car of unorthodox but advanced concept, engaged several of America's top automobile engineers, and leased a Chicago factory where engines for combat aircraft had been produced.

Only 50 cars were built, however, all of them prototypes with varying specifications, before the collapse of what some believed was little more than a publicity stunt, but which others regarded as a brilliant if abortive enterprise.

The Tucker Torpedo embodied many radical features, such as a rear-mounted, flat-Six engine, a special central headlamp which swiveled with the front wheels for illumination on bends, all around independent suspension by self-damping rubber cartridges, and aircraft-type disk brakes.

The engine intended for the car was to be a 9,650-cc

giant cast in aluminum, with hydraulically operated valves in hemispherical heads, direct fuel injection, and sealed cooling. It would turn over at 1,800 rpm and deliver 150 horsepower. High cost, schedules, and circumstance prevented the manufacture of this engine in any quantity, and, instead, a light alloy, overhead valve helicopter engine built by Aircooled Motors (formerly the Franklin Company) was adapted, being converted to water cooling in the process. Total capacity of its six horizontally opposed cylinders was 5,500 cc, and the power, at first 150 horsepower, was later brought up to 166 horsepower.

Prototype tests established that the Tucker Torpedo was excellent on roadholding and had a maximum speed of over 115 mph. Its transmission was to have been automatic, incorporating a hydraulic torque convertor; but like the engine, this could not be perfected in the tense circumstances under which the car was developed.

Temporary substitutes varied on different prototypes; some had manual gearboxes, others electrically controlled pre-selector boxes, and another an automatic system called the "Tuckermatic." Wheelbase of the Torpedo was 130 inches, track 65 inches.

Anticipating modern safety demands with uncanny precision, Tucker prescribed crash padding all around, recessed door handles, plexiglass mirror, and pop-out windshield. A collapsible steering column and safety belts were also projected, but deep financial problems brought this far-seeing enterprise to a sad halt in 1949.

This remarkable car incorporated several ideas that are still new today—for example the padded dashboard (top left) and the central swiveling headlamp, which followed the steering (above). The rear-mounted engine has six horizontally opposed cylinders and 166 horsepower output.

INDIANAPOLIS MOTOR SPEEDWAY MUSEUM

INDIANAPOLIS

most of which can claim to have won the 500 at least once.

There is the Marmon that won the first race in 1911, driven by Ray Harroun, one of the unforgettable Millers, Wilbur Shaw's famous 3-liter Maserati, and the very successful Kurtis Krafts of the 1950s. And there are some cars that, though they did not race at Indianapolis, are nevertheless of considerable interest. For instance, the museum owns the first American gas turbine car, the General Motors XP21 Firebird with Boeing power unit, along with the white and blue 3-liter Duesenberg with which Jimmy Murphy scored an unforgettable American victory in the French Grand Prix of 1921.

Even if not all the Indianapolis winners are present, there are many interesting drawings and photographs, cups and medals to fill in the picture, and unusual exhib-

its including the first safety helmet used by an American racing driver. The museum is open throughout the year from 9 A.M. to 5 P.M., and entry is free.

Of course, the ideal visiting time is May, when the roar and whine from the nearby track lends new life to the racing cars of the past, recalling the great ones that tasted victory—and the ones that only tried, such as the fabulous Novis, with their centrifugal superchargers that rent the air with their thunderous exhaust note, and the shrill humming of the gas turbine-powered cars, which a few years back came so close to eclipsing the piston-engined cars.

A vast amount of enthralling speed history is recalled in this unique museum dedicated exclusively to racing cars. The organizers are always out to augment their collection and expect to enlarge the building eventually.

Marmon Wasp

1911

The great Indianapolis Speedway had been opened for racing two years earlier, but it was not until 1911 that the surfacing and other details were completed to the organizers' full satisfaction, enabling them to promote their first major event, the Indianapolis 500. It proved a highly successful meeting, particularly for the Marmon Wasp, the car that won the race.

The Marmon Company had its factory in Indianapolis, and like everyone else was anxious to win the race because of its enormous publicity value. Although he had already announced his retirement from racing, Marmon's designer-driver, Ray Harroun, was persuaded to drive the single-seater Wasp with which he had already won a shorter race at Indianapolis the previous year.

The Marmon Wasp is a large vehicle with an in-line, six-cylinder, water-cooled engine. This has side valves in a T-head, and the bore and stroke of 114.3x127 mm give

a total engine capacity of 7,820 cc. The power output was never declared, but it must have been about 100 horsepower or perhaps even more. The specification includes a single carburetor, a Rémy magneto (by the factory that later became Delco-Rémy), and force-feed lubrication.

The Wasp's frame consists of two longitudinal members and transverse bracing, and the suspension is by semi-elliptic leaf springs at the front and by full-elliptics at the rear, following Marmon production pattern. Firestone tires were used, 34x4.50-inch at the front and 35x5-inch at the rear, on artillery wheels fitted with disks inside and out. The brakes are on the rear wheels only—the circuit was never hard on these components. The Wasp's wheelbase is 116 inches and the tracks are 56 inches both fore and aft.

For a racing car it was notably substantial; even the dry weight was 3,850 pounds, while with the driver in the cockpit and the tank filled with fuel it scaled 4,400 pounds or well above the regulation minimum of 2,350 pounds. Its most interesting feature is the single-seater body, anticipating the European Monopostos of the 1930s by 20 years.

Harroun's decision not to carry a mechanic brought objections from other drivers, who claimed there was no one to warn him of cars coming up behind. He countered by fitting a 20x7-inch mirror in front of his seat—claimed to be the first use of a rear-view mirror in racing.

This is the car that won the very first Indianapolis 500, staged in 1911. Built from parts of the standard production Marmon, it has a large, six-cylinder, side-valve engine of 7.8 liters, fitted into a special narrow chassis carrying one of the earliest single-seater bodies to be built for racing, and a rear-view mirror.

287

Miller-Hartz Special

1932

Harry Miller was one of the greatest American constructors of racing cars. In the late 1920s and early 1930s his cars were not only supreme in the United States, but also showed they could measure up to their European contemporaries on sheer speed. Miller introduced front-wheel drive cars to Indianapolis in 1924, and for several years the system seemed most suitable for the famous race, which this Miller-Hartz Special, driven by Harry Hartz, won in 1932.

Miller was a specialist in engines and mechanical elements of all kinds and, therefore, the chassis of this car was built to his design by Wetteroth, for Harry Hartz. To transmit the drive through the front wheels (which also, of course, steer), Miller adapted the old-time de Dion-type axle, in the form of a stout tube ahead of the axle line, curving back at both ends to support the hub bearers. By this means the line of the drive shafts from the

This front-drive Miller, unlike most Indianapolis cars, is fitted with brakes to the front as well as to the rear wheels—but they are on the inner end of the drive shafts and are not in the actual wheel as it would appear, the apparent drums being housings for the transmission joints. With a different nose this car won the 500 in 1932.

gearbox-cum-differential to the wheels is left unimpeded; the axle is suspended by double reversed quarter-elliptic leaf springs and struts, while the light tubular rear axle has semi-elliptic springs.

Unusually for an Indianapolis car, there are drum brakes all around; those at the front are mounted inboard on the differential housing, while the rear brakes are on the wheels. The quick-release wire wheels are fitted with Firestone 20x6.00-inch racing tires all around.

The Miller-Hartz's engine is a beautifully built, light alloy straight-Eight with twin overhead camshafts and dry sump lubrication, the 73.025x88.9-mm bore and stroke give a total displacement of 2,979 cc. Four downdraft carburetors made by the Miller Company itself are fitted, and ignition is by Bosch high-tension magneto. Curiously, this particular engine was built to the order of Harry Hartz at a time when the Miller works were concentrating on their new four-cylinder engine, forerunner of the famous Offenhauser; in consequence the Hartz engine was built in considerable haste, essentially just enlarging the design of the 1.5-liter "91" engine. Yet this was the engine that won the 500!

Wheelbase is 102 inches and both tracks measure 52 inches. The two-seater bodywork has been modified from its original 1932 form, having a different radiator grille and tail. Maximum speed was nearly 140 mph.

Maserati 8CTF Boyle Special

1938

Maserati is the only Italian make that has managed to win the Indianapolis 500, and this happened two years running in 1939 and 1940, when the American Wilbur Shaw drove a 1938 Type 8CTF to victory.

It is a lovely car with the classic lines of the period just before World War II. It is powered by a water-cooled, straight-Eight engine with a 69-mm bore and 100-mm stroke (not to be confused with the later eight-cylinder, 3-liter Maserati, which had "square" 78x78-mm dimensions). Total cylinder capacity is 2,992 cc, and the maximum power output on alcohol was about 350 horsepower at 6,000 rpm.

The two blocks of four cylinders are cast iron with integral heads, while the crankcase and sump are of light alloy. The twin overhead camshafts are gear-driven off the front of the engine, ignition is by Scintilla Vertex magneto, and there is dry sump lubrication with an oil

The lovely lines of this 3-liter, eight-cylinder Maserati make it one of the classic racing cars. It is the only Italian car ever to have won the Indianapolis race—and it did it twice, in 1939 and 1940.

cooler; the actual oil tank is fitted between the chassis below the cockpit, where it acts as the central transverse member of the chassis. Two superchargers with two Memini carburetors are mounted at the front of the engine, being driven off the crankshaft.

The chassis is a very simple structure, with two parallel side members and transverse bracing welded in place. Front suspension is independent by wishbones and torsion bars, while the rigid (non-independent) rear axle is underslung, suspended by quarter-elliptic springs, and located by oval torque arms. Large-diameter drum brakes on all four wheels are of Lockheed hydraulic type.

The Maserati's quick-release wire wheels have Duralumin rims for lightness, and carry Firestone racing tires measuring 5.50x19 inches at the front and 6.50x19 inches at the rear. The wheelbase is 107 inches, the front track is 52.8 inches, and the rear is 53.5 inches. Total weight in track trim is about 1,720 pounds.

Somewhat wasted at Indianapolis was the Maserati's road racing type four-speed gearbox; this is in unit with the engine, the drive being transmitted to the rear axle via a torque tube-enclosed propeller shaft. The clutch was of multiple-disk type.

The 8CTF's fuel tank holds 40 gallons (150 liters) of fuel mixture, enough for little more than 125 miles (200 km) at racing speeds. The maximum speed of the car at Indianapolis is given as about 162 mph.

Kurtis-Offenhauser Fuel Injection Special

1953

The Fuel Injection Special with which Bill Vukovich won the 1953 Indianapolis 500 can be considered representative of a whole era of Indianapolis racing—the period that runs from the end of World War II to the 1960s, when the European technique of the rear engine finally took root in the United States and ousted what had been the typical American front-engined roadster.

This car, like the vast majority that have raced at Indianapolis, embodies in its title the name of the sponsor financing its participation for advertising purposes. The cult of the sponsored Indianapolis "Special" began in the mid-1920s, and by the 1930s it had become the custom for the sponsor to be almost anyone from a soap factory or some food or drinks firm to a car accessories manufacturer. So the Fuel Injection Special entered by an injection specialist has a chassis built by Kurtis Kraft, who was a specialist in racing chassis and a

This is a typical Indianapolis roadster, popular into the 1960s, when it was ousted by the rear-engined cars. Although old-fashioned in general appearance, this was a very fast car with which Bill Vukovich won the 1953 Indianapolis 500 at 128.74 mph.

Meyer-Drake Offenhauser engine, that classic Indianapolis source of power.

This engine, designed by Leo Goossen 22 years earlier and generally referred to as the Offy, is a big four-cylinder with really exceptional dimensions of 111.125x114.3-mm bore and stroke and 4,434.2-cc capacity; the displacement of a single cylinder—1,100 cc—indicates what a giant it is. It has twin overhead camshafts, four valves per cylinder, indirect fuel injection, and an estimated 400-horsepower output at 6,500 rpm in 1953 form. It runs on a ferocious diet of alcohol and nitromethane, and the power has been continually increased until today, with a turbocharger, it produces a fantastic 900-plus horsepower!

As used in the 1953 Kurtis, the Offy 270 is mounted at the front and inclined at 36 degrees to the right side of the car; this is to reduce both the frontal area and the center of gravity. It drives through a multiple-plate clutch and a two-speed gearbox, which amounts to a "low" for getting under way after pit stops, and a direct drive, which is used constantly at high speed.

A truss-type tubular frame is used, and it is interesting that, after employing independent front suspension on their earlier cars, Kurtis should revert to a non-independent, tubular front axle, sprung by crossed torsion bars, on this car. At the rear the rigid axle is suspended on parallel torsion bars, with radius arms running forward. The brakes are still only on the rear wheels, and the light alloy wheels with quick-release center wing nuts have Firestone tires, 7.10x16 inches at the front and 8.00x18 inches at the rear. Considering the size of the car (95-inch wheelbase), the weight is fairly low at 1,625 pounds; maximum speed was well over 155 mph.

SMITHSONIAN INSTITUTION

The Smithsonian Institution is an outstanding example of a technical institute established by a bequest or foundation. English scientist James Smithson died in 1829, leaving £105,000 to his nephew with the proviso that if *he* died without heir the sum would pass to the United States Government to found an institution in Washington "for the increase and diffusion of knowledge among men."

The bequest was accepted by the U. S. in 1838, the Institution was duly founded, and subsequently augmented by other bequests and donations. Today the Smithsonian complex includes the museum proper, an astrophysical observatory, a large zoo, and several famous art collections. Each year more than 20 million people visit the grounds, which cover an area equal to twelve city blocks. The oldest building, the administrative office, was

WASHINGTON

built between 1847 and 1855 of gray stone with echoes of classical Greek and Roman styles. Then came the Science and Industries building in 1881, the Natural History block in 1911, and two buildings housing art collections that date from 1921 and 1941.

In 1964 work began on an imposing new structure for the Museum of History and Technology, which houses the transportation exhibits. Automobiles are only a part of the collection, which also includes aircraft and boats. The plane in which Charles Lindbergh made his famous transatlantic flight to Paris is particularly exciting.

About fifty self-propelled vehicles are displayed, ranging from bicycles and steam and gas-powered tricycles through cars of all ages, up to the 1964 turbine-driven Chrysler, and covering all stages of land locomotion and all methods of propulsion—

steam, electricity and gasoline. Most of the vehicles exhibited are extremely rare specimens, and their quality and interest value make up for the small quantity. The oldest motorized vehicle of all at the museum is the Roper steam velocipede of about 1869. Although this looks as if it came straight from one of the cartoons of the period in which the mechanical horses are shown spitting out smoke, it is an extremely ingenious device, and one remarkably well engineered for the period.

Every vehicle on display is of American origin. Although certain early European cars are fundamental to the overall history of the automobile, the American cars exhibited are the really classic ones, including examples of Duryea, Winton, Pierce-Arrow, White Steamer, Cadillac and other makes of significance in U.S. motoring history.

Simplex 50-hp

1912

Support for three spare wheels is provided by the large metal well at the rear (left). The curious cylinders on the spring shackles are a form of shock absorber. The Simplex was one of the United States' finest makes.

Simplex, an American quality make built on East 83 Street, New York, operated from 1907 until the mid-1920s; the 1912 50-hp two-seater to be seen at the Smithsonian represents one of the finest models. Its big four-cylinder, in-line, 9,777.5-cc engine has a 146x146-mm bore and stroke, and the effective power must have been considerably more than the rated 50 horsepower—probably about 75 horsepower.

This engine is of T-head type, with the twin side camshafts in the crankcase operating the inlet valves on one side and the exhaust valves on the other. The exhaust camshaft can be moved lengthwise by a handle under the radiator to optional settings, one partially raising the exhaust valves and thus reducing the compression to make starting easier, the other for normal driving.

The crankcase is of cast aluminum; dual ignition is by a Bosch twin magneto and two spark plugs to each cylinder, and cooling is by a handsome Mercedes-style radiator, a water pump driven off the distributor, and a flywheel fan. Lubrication is on the total loss system; a small oil reservoir on the dash supplies oil to the various points that need it by means of a gear pump. The main oil tank, holding no less than 13 gallons, is at the rear, mounted between the two seats and a 40-gallon cylindrical fuel tank.

The Simplex's extremely sturdy channel-section steel chassis has a lengthy wheelbase of 130 inches, and the axles have semi-elliptic leaf spring suspension, aided by early telescopic shock absorbers called "jounce preventers." The rebuilt artillery-type wheels with demountable rims are fitted with 23x5-inch Firestone "non-skid" tires, which are somewhat fat for the period, spoiling the authenticity of the restoration.

Transmission is through a multi-plate clutch, mounted inside the flywheel, to a separate four-speed gearbox,

The Simplex at the Smithsonian is the "fast" type with a powerful 9.7-liter engine able to propel it at 75 mph. Its speedster body was built by Holbrook. Simplex was among the last to use chain drive.

which is combined with the differential in a large aluminum case. From there, drive to the rear wheels is by side chains. Simplex was one of the last American manufacturers to maintain chain-drive transmission, long after the drive shaft had become normal practice. There are adjustable radius rods at each end of the rear axle to allow fore-and-aft movement to keep the chains properly tensioned.

The rakish speedster body on the Smithsonian's Simplex was made by Holbrook, a well-known New York coachbuilder. It is extremely simple, with no windshield and three spare wheels strapped onto the back of the fuel tank. The big headlights are acetylene-powered, but Dietz combination electric-kerosene sidelights are fitted. There is a manometer on the wooden dashboard, to indicate the pressure in the gas and oil tanks, and a Warner speedometer. Cars of this type were capable of 75 mph or over and were frequently and successfully raced.

THE MUSEUM OF AUTOMOBILES

The Museum of Automobiles in Morrilton, Arkansas, one of the numerous private collections in the United States, houses the cars belonging to two enthusiastic collectors, George Waterman and the late Winthrop Rockefeller. Although the collection is not large, it is well worth visiting for the cars have all been carefully restored.

The Rockefeller collection consists chiefly of classic road cars and early Americans such as Duryea, Winton, Mitchell, Lozier and others that have gone forever. The Waterman collection includes a series of unique racing cars of the pre-World War I period. Besides the four racing machines shown on following pages, there is a 1908 Isotta-Fraschini, one of the few surviving intact from the early years of this make, a very old Panhard dated 1892, a 1907 Rolls-Royce Silver Ghost, a 1911 FIAT and later cars, including examples of Stutz and Mercedes-Benz.

The rectangular building itself is most

unusual, and probably unique: although it covers over 2,000 square yards it has absolutely no internal columns. The whole roof structure is suspended from a series of outside pillars that are buttressed by four corner structures, so that the ceiling of the huge single hall resembles a great canvas gracefully sheltering the mechanical glories of the past from wind and rain.

This modern building stands in a tourists' paradise in the mountain and forest landscape of the Petit Jean National Park, and is one of the attractions for visitors to the park. A special feature at the museum every June is a rally of old cars, during which there are races, *concours d'élégance* and competitions for the finest examples of restoration and so on. Several of the museum exhibits are given an airing and in this way are kept alive.

The Arkansas collection is one of the most recently opened automotive museums, for the Rockefeller collection was bought from the collector James Melton in 1960, and has been augmented since then. The oldest car is that 1892 Panhard, and the most recent dates from 1941. A good third of the cars on view are, in fact, non-American, but the restorations are highly effective, helped, no doubt, by the proximity of a special concern, PJA Pneumatic, which specializes in making obsolete patterned tires for vintage cars.

Although the Arkansas museum stands in the heart of beautiful woodland, it is easily accessible, not only by car (it lies just off Route 40 near the little town of Morrilton) but even by plane, as there is a small private airport close by.

Not far away lies the Winthrop Rockefeller estate. For visitors there are hotel and motel accommodations nearby, and numerous other tourist attractions exist, such as the splendid local flora and fauna. All this makes Morrilton something different from other automobile museums

Gordon Bennett Napier

1903

Montague Napier and S. F. Edge made history by developing and marketing the world's first successful six-cylinder engine car, but the Napier make was also famous for some outstanding racing achievements, including the winning of the 1902 Gordon Bennett Cup race. The model in the Arkansas museum has only

In this car, as with others in the Morrilton collection, one hesitates whether to admire more the original craftsmanship or the careful restoration. Did this Gordon Bennett Napier ever look so pristine back in 1903 when it was built? Note the beautifully made radiator.

four cylinders, but is one of the oldest surviving cars made by the Napier firm and is the oldest English racing car in existence today.

It was one of three Napiers built for the fourth Gordon Bennett race in 1903 and was the car driven by famous British racing pioneer Charles Jarrott. Unfortunately he crashed dramatically early in the race when his steering broke, the car charged a bank and overturned. Jarrott and his mechanic, who had been strapped in and was trapped beneath the car, were left for dead but fortunately lived to tell the tale.

The Napier's in-line, four-cylinder, engine is in two blocks of two cylinders; it has a bore and stroke of 139.7x127 mm and a displacement of 7,708 cc. Its 45 horsepower was reached at about 1,000 rpm, and the maximum speed was about 65 mph. Cooling is by water and a honeycomb radiator, and gravity lubrication is employed. The inlet valves are automatically operated by suction, a system largely abandoned elsewhere for mechanical operation, and the exhaust valves are operated by a side-mounted camshaft.

Transmission is by a leather-covered cone clutch, a separate three-speed gearbox, and propeller shaft final drive, which was cleaner and quieter than chains.

This compact car could travel at 65 mph and weighed about 2,420 pounds. The picture on the left shows the water pump, driven by friction from the flywheel. The lubricators on the dashboard were directly operated by the driver or mechanic during the race. Headlamps could be mounted on the front forks when required. This was probably the first British car to wear British racing green in a race.

Yet another instance that the 1903 Napier was a mixture of advanced and dated features lies in its chassis, which is of armored wood; that is, ash reinforced with steel plates, a practice superseded by pressed-steel side members on most racing cars by that time. The rigid axles are suspended by semi-elliptic leaf springs at the front and rear, and there are external contracting band brakes on the transmission and rear wheels.

The Napier has a 94-inch wheelbase and 54-inch tracks front and rear, while the weight is approximately 2,420 pounds. The wooden artillery-type wheels have twelve spokes at the rear and only ten at the front, and are equipped with Dunlop 875x105 tires. The round bolster tank at the rear was fitted subsequent to 1903, while for some reason the Arkansas museum shows the car fitted with ugly front fenders, which it certainly did not wear in the 1903 Gordon Bennett race.

Renault Grand Prix Replica

1907

In this 1907 Renault racing car can be seen many of the characteristics of the production model Renaults that the famous firm from Billancourt, Paris was building in that period. In particular, the "coal scuttle" hood and the radiator mounted behind the engine, protruding on both sides of the hood, were always strong Renault features. There was reason behind them: the dashboard radiator ensured efficient thermosiphon cooling, and thus the water pump, a frequent cause of trouble in racing, could be done away with.

Based on the 90-horsepower Renault that won the French Grand Prix in 1906 and finished second in 1907, the Replica models built for the U.S. market used higher chassis with straight side rails and 35-horsepower four-cylinder engines with a displacement of 7.25 liters. There are two blocks of two cylinders, cast in iron in a single piece with the head, mounted on an aluminum

crankcase. A Renault carburetor is used, lubrication is by a simple yet effective gravity system, and ignition is by Bosch high-tension magneto with automatic advance.

Like the 1903 Gordon Bennett Napier described previously, this Renault has a leather-covered cone-type clutch and a three-speed plus reverse gearbox separate from the engine. Again like the Napier, final drive is by propeller shaft, at a time when side chains were prevalent, especially on racing cars. Right from the make's inception in 1898, no Renault car ever had chain drive. The car in the Morrilton collection has a differential, but it is interesting that for long-distance road races this was often eliminated.

The chassis has pressed-steel longitudinal members,

The top picture bears witness to the might of the early engines. The Renault's two blocks of two cylinders are set off smartly by gleaming brass and copper pipes. The tube on the right houses the plug leads. This 7.25-liter, side-valve unit was simple and accessible.

well-braced crosswise, and the suspension is by semi-elliptic leaf springs to both axles, with the addition of friction shock absorbers, an early instance of their use on a racing car. The artillery-type wheels have wooden spokes and detachable iron rims, and carry non-original 870x90 tires at the front and 880x120 at the rear. The footbrake operates on the rear drums and the handbrake on the transmission just aft of the gearbox.

As befits a racing car, the bodywork is minimal, amounting to two seats and a rear-mounted fuel tank with spare wheels strapped to it. Replica GP Renaults of this kind won two 24-hour races in the United States in 1907 and 1909.

The neat row of lubricators (below) is arranged on the dash so that they can be checked and adjusted by the driver or his riding mechanic. Touring Renaults also had this feature. At the top, the tap for draining the dashboard-type radiator. Although the Replica Grand Prix Renault weighed about 2,200 pounds, it could reach a speed of over 90 mph.

Grand Prix
Benz
1908

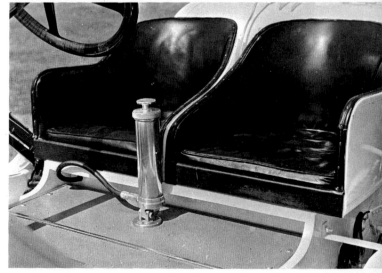

The Benz cars built for the 1908 Grand Prix at Dieppe were very representative of racing practice of the time; they were big and brawny, with massive engines, chain drive, and no streamlining. The white-painted cars did not manage to win the race, but they came in second (after being in the lead at one stage), third, and seventh, which was a fine team achievement. One of the cars survived the years and recently has been a prized exhibit at the Morrilton museum.

The design of this car is traditional in concept, with the large four-cylinder engine in two blocks of two cylinders. It has a bore of 155 mm, in keeping with the regulations of the day, which in conjunction with a 165-mm stroke gives the impressive overall capacity of 12,453 cc. Its maximum revolutions were high for the time at 1,650 rpm, and the power output was about 120 horsepower. The car was timed at close to 100 mph during the race.

There is stark purpose in every line of the Grand Prix Benz. The hand-operated fuel pump is placed vertically between the two bucket seats. The effective white finish is Germany's official racing color.

The overhead valves are pushrod-and-rocker-arm operated from a camshaft housed in the crankcase. A Bosch high-tension magneto is used, the carburetor is of Benz manufacture, lubrication is by gravity and splash, and water cooling is through a honeycomb radiator, centrifugal water pump, and fan.

The GP Benz's transmission is typical of the period, with leather-covered cone clutch and a short drive shaft connected to the single casing that houses both the gears and final drive incorporating the differential. There are four speeds and reverse, and the drive to the rear wheels is by side chains and large-diameter sprockets, which are liberally drilled for lightness.

Two pressed-steel longitudinal members form the chassis, with some vital cross-bracing provided by the engine and gearbox. Wheelbase of the car is 52 inches and the tracks at front and rear are 109 inches. The suspension on the two rigid axles is by semi-elliptic leaf springs; the rear axle has adjustable torque arms.

Artillery-type wooden wheels are fitted, but the tires which are American reproductions with non-skid treads, cannot be described as authentic; in the Grand Prix the Benz team used German Continental tires. Apart from this flaw, the car at Morrilton very closely resembles the Grand Prix Benz in the form in which

the French driver Victor Héméry drove it in the American Grand Prize races at Savannah in 1908, 1910, and 1911.

A study in power—the tall, imposing 2.5-liter engine of the Grand Prix Benz. Clearly to be seen are the overhead valves operated by long pushrods and rocker arms, and the dual ignition by twin Bosch magnetos and two spark plugs to each cylinder. Note how far apart the two banks of two cylinders are on this power unit. The top photograph shows the four engine lubricators, which could be adjusted one by one.

Grand Prix Mercedes

1908

Of the many Mercedes racing cars, this is one of the oldest and also one of the most famous. It was one of a team of three that ran in the 1908 Grand Prix at Dieppe, one of them winning in the hands of Christian Lautenschlager, while another was placed fifth, and the third set the fastest lap of the whole race.

As can be seen from the magnificent example in the Morrilton museum, it is a superbly proportioned machine in the classic idiom. Regulations for the race laid down a 155-mm maximum bore limit for four-cylinder engines, and Mercedes chose dimensions of

155x170-mm bore and stroke (12,781 cc) for two of their cars, and 155x180 mm (13,533 cc) for the third. Maximum power was about 135 horsepower at 1,400 rpm for both sizes, and the maximum speed was about 103 mph. The engine is formed in two blocks of two cylinders with fixed heads, and there are two side camshafts in the crankcase, one on the offside operating overhead inlet valves through pushrods and rockers, and one on the nearside operating the side exhaust valves. The camshafts are driven by exposed gears at the rear of the engine. Ignition is by Bosch high-tension magneto, and carburetion by a Maybach instrument. Oil from a large tank under the cowl was pumped to the upper parts of the engine, which relied otherwise on gravity to do its job. The crankshaft runs in three bearings, and cooling is by honeycomb radiator, pump, and fan.

The clutch is an all-metal scroll-type patented by Daimler, and the four-speed gearbox is separate from the engine and in unit with the differential and cross shaft carrying the driving sprockets (drilled for lightness) for the side chains to the rear wheels.

The Mercedes chassis has pressed-steel side members and cross-bracing riveted in. Suspension of the rigid axles at front and rear is by conventional semi-elliptic leaf springs, assisted by friction shock absorbers, but the whole car is engineered to Mercedes' highest standards to ensure complete race-worthiness. The artillery-type wood-spoked wheels have detachable rims. Once again, authenticity of a historic car has been marred by fitting wrong-sized tires; those on the car today are 895x135s, whereas the original sizes used in 1908 were 825x105 front and 880x125 rear.

Braking is on the rear wheels only, with internal expanding drum brakes operated by the hand lever and a transmission brake operated by pedal. Wheelbase is 106 inches, both tracks are 55.5 inches, and the weight of the cars varied from 2,540 pounds to 2,865 pounds, depending on chassis reinforcement. It is believed that the car at Morrilton was that raced in the 1908 Grand Prix by Otto Salzer.

The Mercedes looked very much like its rival and compatriot, the Benz, built for the same 1908 French Grand Prix. Driver and mechanic on the Mercedes enjoyed better cockpit protection, however, while the extra 15 horsepower under the hood brought it victory over the Benz and other rivals. Note the extra fuel tank (right) installed in front of the driver's and mechanic's seats and molded to serve as a leg rest.

INDEX